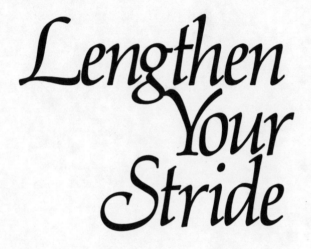

Lengthen Your Stride

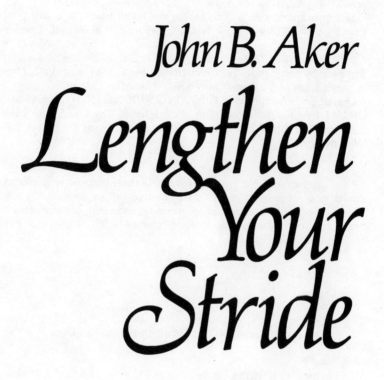

John B. Aker

Lengthen Your Stride

Fleming H. Revell
Old Tappan, New Jersey

Library of Congress Cataloging-in-Publication Data

Aker, John B.
    Lengthen your stride : improving your walk with God / John B. Aker.
        p.   cm.
    ISBN 0-8007-1550-0
    1. Aker, John B. 2. Evangelical Free Church of America—Clergy— Biography. 3. Ex-monks—United States—Biography. 4. Christian life—1960-   I. Title.
BX7548.Z8A783 1988
289.8—dc19   88-18245
[B]   CIP

TO Dad,
whose greatest ambition is expressed in the words of
Joshua:

"... As for me and my house,
we will serve the Lord"

and who was so instrumental in seeing his family become
part of the household of faith before he was called home
on August 13, 1987 ...

and Mom,
whose more than fifty loving years with Dad evidenced
the truth:

"An excellent wife is
the crown of her husband ..."

and who continues enthusiastically to expend all her energies in the care of her family and the church of her Lord
as she eagerly awaits the homeward call of the Master.

Acknowledgments

Alone at a mountain retreat provided me by my brother, I struggled long days and, seemingly, even longer nights with the first seven chapters of this book. It was a far greater task than I ever dreamed. In fact, I wanted to take the manuscript and the tapes and throw them to the wind. . . .

At that point, Chuck Swindoll called. As I poured out my frustration with _my book_, Chuck laughed and said simply: "Aker, it sounds like you are in labor and about to deliver!"

The thought of being _about to deliver_ got me through the next several days. But the feeling of wanting to quit returned many times. And I probably would have—had it not been for some very special people to whom I am indebted:

Dad,
who read and initially edited all
but the last chapter.

Mom,
who cheered me on and then read the
last chapter in Dad's place.

Alan and Irene,
my brother and sister, who have invested
so much of their lives in mine and then
allowed me to share some of them with you.

Frank D'Angelo and Len Freeman,
friends who believe in me and
wanted to see the story told.

John Andersen and Bob Hagman,
two of my elders at Montvale Evangelical
Free Church, who never doubted the importance
of this project and its benefits in the
overall life of our local assembly.

David Fisher and John Vawter,
my brothers in pastoral ministry, to whom I am
accountable and who remained excited about the
book even when it seemed to really depress me.

Chuck Swindoll,
who challenged me to write, sent my first
attempts to Fleming Revell, and then
laughed every time I wanted to cry.

Bill,
just Bill, a friend, who gave me so much of
his time and wisdom as he interacted with
every page . . . every paragraph.

Joy Asp,
my administrative assistant and friend who typed
and retyped, and then typed again page after page
and helped me believe, through her smiles, it was
all worth it.

Laura, Natalie, and Jana,
our daughters, whose love for the Master and
walk with Him is a continuing challenge to
integrity and authenticity in my own life.

Rose,
my loving wife, and best friend, whose greatest
desire is to glorify the Lord as we seek, together,
to *lengthen our stride.* . . .

Contents

_____ *Foreword*

A journey, like love, is a many-splendored thing.

We encounter the unexpected along the way, which surprises us. We learn lessons as we adapt to certain stresses and hardships, which stretch us. We happen upon scenes that span the extremes from the monotonous to the magnificent, which prompt us to respond in spontaneous ways. It forces us out of our own little worlds and awakens us to dimensions we would not otherwise acknowledge.

The book you hold in your hands is the journal of one man's journey. It is a fascinating journey full of surprises and struggles, some of which will make you weep, others of which will make you smile, all of which will make you think. This is no lighthearted fantasy designed to entertain you. It is an authentic account of the extent to which an individual will go to find peace deep within.

The best part of all is that the main Character is unseen but never absent. His voice is inaudible, but it is not silent. His power, though profoundly evident, is agonizingly subtle, yet on other occasions frighteningly stormy. The Passionist monk who began this journey could well have sat for the portrait William Cowper painted with his pen:

God moves in a mysterious way,
His wonders to perform;
He plants His footsteps in the sea,
And rides upon the storm.

Deep in unfathomable mines
Of never-failing skill
He treasures up His bright designs,
And works His sovereign will.

Judge not the Lord by feeble sense,
But trust Him for His grace;
Behind a frowning Providence
He hides a smiling face.

It has been my delight to know John Aker well over a decade. For most of those years I have urged him to tell his story. It seemed a shame for him to keep the secrets of his pilgrimage to himself. They are far too significant to remain hidden in the creases of his brilliant mind. His pursuit of God, which he recounts so well, is a captivating one. More importantly, it is a bold reminder that God is still at work. His hand on a life may be invisible and mysterious, but it is never feeble or unsure; He knows what He is about. What hope that brings! If He can change the heart of a monk, disciplined to the core and stubbornly religious, He is able to go to the outermost limits and work His sovereign will in other lives as well . . . even yours and mine.

This fascinating journey, therefore, should interest everyone but surprise no one. It is another account of divine love once again stooping down in time and space, touching and transforming a life through irresistible grace. It happens every day. Love, that many-splendored thing, never fails.

CHARLES R. SWINDOLL
Pastor, author, radio Bible teacher

Introduction

Seeking God

On a high holy day—the Feast of Mary's Assumption into heaven, August 15, 1962—as I walked down the long aisle of the Monastery Church of Saint Paul of the Cross, warm and precious memories flashed across my mind. The awareness that I had reached a significant milestone in my studies for the priesthood greatly moved me. With cross on my shoulder and crown of thorns on my head, I knelt before Father Rector at the high altar. Slowly and somberly, I professed my vows:

> I, Confrater André of Our Lady of The Holy Cross, do vow and promise, by a simple vow and promise to Almighty God, to Blessed Mary, ever a virgin, to all the heavenly court, and to you Father, poverty, chastity, and obedience, as also a diligent endeavor to promote, according to my strength, in the hearts of the faithful, devotion to the Passion of Our Lord, according to the Rules and Constitution of the Discalced Clerics of the Most Holy Cross and Passion of Our Lord Jesus Christ. . . .

It was done! I was a Passionist monk. . . .

On just another such day—nothing very special about it, March 30, 1968—as we left the dining-room table and walked into the living room with our hosts, a storm of

doubt and despair raged within me. The awful realization
that I had succeeded in making a terrible mess of my life
struck me. With trials and troubles heavy on my mind and
heart, I knelt beside my wife, near the couch. Softly and
simply I prayed:

> Lord Jesus, I need You. I open the door of my life and
> take You as Lord and Savior. Thank You for dying on the
> Cross for me . . . and thank You for forgiving me my sins.
> Take control of the throne of my life and make me the kind
> of person You want me to be. I can't do it on my own. . . .

It was done. I was a child of God. . . .

As I pen these words, the high emotional excitement of
these two events again overwhelms me. The first, an expression of discipline—in a very long direction—I eagerly
embraced. For eight years, I invested all my youthful energies toward that profession of vows. The second event,
a completely unexpected encounter with grace, I earnestly
evaded. Following more than five years of confusion, and
without warning, divine energy impacted my life and
prompted this confession of faith.

These two expressions of faith commitment are very
distinct. I will not—I cannot—denigrate my profession of
vows. Yet I recognize that my confession of faith marked
an even greater change in my life's orientation than those
earlier vows binding me to my monastic community. Both
are fully part of the pursuit. . . .

Shortly after taking Christ as Lord, I began to receive
invitations from Protestant churches to *share my testimony.*
Well, I didn't even know what a testimony was—let alone
know I had one to share! Evidently an awful lot of people
wanted to hear the story of how an ex-monk and ex-intel-
ligence agent came to a saving knowledge of Christ. At
first the countless opportunities to speak across the country, in churches large and small, from so many different
denominations, were frightening . . . then very rewarding
. . . and finally they became more and more difficult each

time. I distinctly remember leaving one such meeting with my wife, Rose, and remarking that I just could not tell the story anymore. People had great interest in the ex-monk and ex-spy aspect of it all, but allowed me very little time to declare the excellencies of this One who so wondrously changed my life. I resolved that night to preach Christ and to use my life and life experiences only as an illustration of His ongoing grace toward me.

Since that time Christ has continued to enrich my life through the people whose lives have intersected with mine. Some have encouraged me to tell the story once again—to speak of the long pursuit.

Part of me says it's not really one story, but three. The first about a young man entering the monastery . . . the second of a man coming to the end of his own strength and meeting an Omnipotent God . . . and the third of all God is doing in reshaping that man—unfit as he is—for His plan and purposes. The pursuit continues.

I still struggle . . . I am not sure such a story has much to say. Yet when I think of all the lives that have impacted mine, I realize it is not simply my story, but the story of many special people whom I have met, who have given me so much of themselves—so much that I needed and continue to need, during this pursuit. . . .

One

Getting Close to God

*T*here we were, three ministers driving out of Minneapolis in a Mercedes-Benz on a balmy Sunday afternoon in January. We hardly knew what to be more thankful for, the Mercedes-Benz or the mild weather.

The car belonged to one of my clerical colleague's parishioners. He had asked us to do him a favor and deliver it in the Chicago area. Since we were going that way anyway, we felt it was "the least we could do."

The trip should have been an enjoyable, eight-hour cruise, but the snow started to fall . . . despite the weather report. Then the windshield wipers forgot they belonged to a Mercedes-Benz and stopped working. A little more than an hour outside Minneapolis, we found ourselves in the midst of a full-blown snowstorm.

We—David Fisher, John Vawter, and I—agreed to take turns driving. When my turn came, I got behind the wheel and drove about a quarter of a mile. Then I convinced my friends that we would all be better off if I got into the backseat and prayed or pulled my jacket over my head. Anything would be better than my driving!

Finally, after passing Madison, Wisconsin, we noticed

an Oldsmobile, pulled off the road and perched precariously on the crest of a small ravine. The car's flashers were blinking; the passengers obviously needed help.

We stopped our Mercedes, and I trudged through the snow to the Olds. I opened the car door to find an elderly couple inside. As the woman stepped out into the snow, she whispered to me, "You've got to help us. My husband had triple bypass surgery a few weeks ago. I need to get him home."

As we helped her husband out, we noticed he was ashen. Obviously, he was not a well man.

Our first thought was to get him to a motel, but the woman said her husband needed his heart medicine, which was at their home in Chicago. So it was imperative that they continue on their way.

We located a wrecker at a nearby service station, and soon their car was pulled out of the ditch. Two of us accompanied them, while the other led the way in the Mercedes.

"What do you do for a living?" the woman soon asked.

"We're ministers," my partner replied.

She seemed relieved. For a while she said nothing. Then she asked another, amazing question: "Do you think it's possible to know God?"

With a question like that to open the conversation, the rest of the journey seemed surprisingly short.

What an important question that is! Do you think it's possible to really know God?

Five months later, almost to the day, I was once again with my two minister friends. Now it was just about summer; we were at the Des Moines airport, to welcome a mutual friend of ours—Charles Swindoll, author, radio speaker, and beloved pastor from Fullerton, California—to a denominational celebration. Chuck had sent each of us a letter, telling us jokingly that we would recognize him at the Des Moines Airport because he would be dressed in a tuxedo, wearing red, hi-top Adidas, and carrying a scarlet Bible under his arm.

We decided he shouldn't be allowed to get away with a joke like that. Although we knew he was only kidding, we decided to go to the airport dressed in black shirts and clerical collars. David Fisher even found a pectoral cross—the cross of a bishop—to wear around his neck. Never had ministers of the Evangelical Free Church been bedecked with such finery.

Unfortunately, Chuck's plane was delayed. Hoping no members of our denomination would recognize us, nervously we went to the coffee shop and tried to find a secluded corner.

As we sipped our coffee, we noticed a middle-aged couple, seated diagonally from us, staring at us. Finally the man said, "Excuse me, gentlemen, are you priests?"

"No," we replied with embarrassment, "we're ministers, not priests."

"Oh, I'm sorry; I thought you might have been priests." He turned away from us as if he were finished speaking, but then spoke again. "The older I get," he said, "the more I really question whether it's even possible to know God."

There it was again.

Knowing God.

For most people that phrase expresses a heart desire, but among evangelicals it has almost become a cliché. As part of our evangelistic technique we ask strangers, "Have you met the Lord?" "Do you know Him? Have you been introduced to Jesus?"

But we also afford people the ease of thinking that once they've met God, they really know Him. Sometimes we relax and tend to believe so ourselves—we think it's all over, when in fact it's just beginning.

Instead of thinking about *knowing God*, I like to think about *intimacy with God*. Our relationship begins when we recognize our need and meet Him, but God has so much more for us than that. He invites us to draw close to Him.

With that invitation, we know God accepts us just as we are. We evangelicals zealously affirm salvation has no conditions. Yet we also know He expects each of us to lead a different kind of life from that time on. The night before He was crucified, Jesus told His disciples, "You are My friends, *if* you do what I command you" (John 15:14, italics added). He predicated acceptance on our willingness to do what He wants us to do.

"No longer do I call you slaves," Jesus continued. "For the slave does not know what his master is doing; but I have called you friends"(v. 15). Our relationship with God is not rooted in servile fear, but in love. Warmth and intimacy exist between God and man.

Inheritance and Experience

Very simply, you can enter into a loving and personal relationship with the God who made, redeemed, and even now sustains you: That is the *way to God*. The Bible speaks of it as the inheritance God bestowed on you at the moment you took Christ as Lord. You can also have a *walk with God:* the experience that ought to be yours if you truly seek to follow Him.

At the moment of salvation, you receive your inheritance, which never changes. Some days you might not feel at all loved, secure, forgiven, adopted, or acceptable. But inheritance does not depend on your emotional state. No matter how you feel, you have the assurance of God's Word that you have been forgiven, will always be loved, and are secure. God alone effects this inheritance—you did nothing to cause the change in your status. Even faith to say yes to the claims of Christ is a gift from the Spirit.

Experience is somewhat different and begins at the moment of conversion. God intends your experience with Him, your intimacy with the Master, to grow . . . to enlarge . . . to change . . . to take on new dimensions as you mature in Him. You affect your experience; sin and the habit of sin can hinder it. Unlike your inheritance, experience is visible to both God and man. When you see someone who knows the depths and the delights of intimacy with the Master, the signs are evident.

Finally, keep in mind that while God has sealed the inheritance, experience opens wide before you. This is the very essence—the stuff—of which intimacy with the Master will be made. And God invites you to be intimate with Him.

The Disposition Toward Intimacy

Unfortunately, not all of us seize the invitation to intimacy. Though a few of us may excuse ourselves on the score that we failed to realize it was there—based solely on His acceptance of us—the rest of us must consider our attitudes toward His gracious invitation.

Personally, we must be disposed toward developing intimacy, but most of us feel quite content with a very small dosage of God. Wilbur Rees was so right:

> I would like to buy $3 worth of God, please. Not enough to explode my soul or disturb my sleep, but just enough to equal a cup of warm milk or a snooze in the sunshine. I don't want enough of Him to make me love a black man or pick beets with a migrant. I want ecstasy, not transformation; I want the warmth of the womb, not a new birth. I want a pound of the Eternal in a paper sack. I would like to buy $3 worth of God, please.

Far more prone to that attitude than we might want to admit, all of us find it just too easy to compartmentalize our lives into a God-kind-of-time and a not-God-kind-of-time.

Because the Psalmist knew that intimacy with the Master has to permeate every facet of our beings, he made that his heart cry: "Who may ascend into the hill of the Lord? And who may stand in His holy place?" (Psalms 24:3). In Psalms 15:1 he asks, "O Lord, who may abide in Thy tent? Who may dwell on Thy holy hill?"

Really both verses ask, "Lord, who can know real intimacy with You?"

Keys to Intimacy

Integrity. The questions asked by the Psalmist have their answers in the verses that immediately follow. Psalms 24:4, 5 answers, "He who has clean hands and a pure heart, Who has not lifted up his soul to falsehood, And has not sworn deceitfully. He shall receive a blessing from the Lord And righteousness from the God of his salvation." The blessing? intimacy with God.

Intimacy is linked with clean hands, a pure heart, and an honest tongue. Psalms 15:2 calls someone like this "he who walks with integrity, and works righteousness. . . ." The person who finds closeness with God is disposed toward integrity: "The crooked man is an abomination to the Lord: But He is intimate with the upright" (Proverbs 3:32).

Several years ago I preached a series of meetings to a congregation in which the pastor and his wife were celebrating their thirty-fifth wedding anniversary. For the occasion the children had gathered and gotten gifts for their parents, including a Bible, in which they had inscribed these words, "A righteous man who walks in his integrity—How blessed are his sons after him" (Proverbs 20:7). When they read that verse in the Sunday-morning service, I felt challenged as never before. In that moment I looked beyond Pastor and Mrs. Gunsolley and saw their children—all four living for the Lord, serving Him vibrantly in their own ministries.

As I thought back to my three girls at home and all the happiness I wanted them to have, chief on the list would be the blessedness of following a man of integrity. But integrity does not come easily to me; in fact it's very difficult.

The kind of integrity I'd like to show is exemplified by a story Chuck Swindoll told me. A pastor making calls on his people somehow got so rushed, preoccupied, or distracted that he completely lost his sense of direction. Pausing to get his bearings, he suddenly realized he was in one of the seamy sections of town. He glanced to his right and saw an adult movie house. Unintentionally his eyes caught the blatantly seductive marquee, and he began to experience the lure and the pull. Within his heart he knew a real temptation to get closer, study the marquee, and even enter the theater. That's when he remembered a line from the hymn he had used to close his Sunday-morning service: "I would be true, for there are those who trust me."

I want that line to be my prayer in the dead of night, when I walk the streets of distant cities. Anytime I could do in secret things that might alter my testimony or affect the opinion of those closest to me, I want the integrity of which that song speaks. Building or keeping intimacy with God requires it.

Sincerity. Psalms 15:2 ends with the description of the second key to intimacy, when it says the person who can abide in the tent of God and dwell on his holy hill "speaks truth in his heart." In all Scripture, only this time does that phrase appear—perhaps because the heart really *doesn't* speak.

But the tongue, the messenger of the heart, relays information from the core of one's being. It shows what we really believe. Solomon talks about this when he says, "As a man thinks within himself, so he is" (*see* Proverbs 23:7).

That doesn't mean every message comes across clearly, though. Even the short distance between the heart and lips can allow for great distortion. Jesus commented on this when He quoted the prophet Isaiah, "This people honors Me with their lips, But their heart is far away from Me" (Matthew 15:8). We can go through all the motions, have all the ritual, use the right language, but if it doesn't flow from deep within, and if sincerity doesn't mark our lives, we cannot have intimacy with God.

If I am sincere with God, I will say to Him, "These are my loves, my desires, and my delights and joys in life. . . ." But I cannot let it stop there. Sincerity must characterize both my relationship with the One who knows when my words and heart don't match as well as my relationship with other people.

Scripture tells us sincerity forms the best basis for a friendship: "Faithful are the wounds of a friend, But deceitful are the kisses of an enemy" (Proverbs 27:6). One who loves you lets you see his heart, saying, "This is how I truly feel." Though those feelings might wound you, a friend will show them to you anyway, if that truth will profit you the most. Beware of the one who tells you all is right when things couldn't be more wrong!

We need to watch the tongue, which can too easily lead us astray. Speaking for the Lord, Solomon says:

> There are six things which the Lord hates, Yes seven which are an abomination to Him: Haughty eyes, a lying tongue, And hands that shed innocent blood, A heart that devises wicked plans, Feet that run rapidly to evil, A false witness who utters lies, And one who spreads strife among brothers.
>
> Proverbs 6:16–19

Later he continues, "A worthless man digs up evil, While his words are as a scorching fire. A perverse man spreads strife, And a slanderer separates intimate friends" (Proverbs 16:27, 28). What damage the tongue can do!

The *Wall Street Journal* (March 12, 1981) carried a special piece that talked about this:

The Snake That Poisons
Everybody

It
topples
governments,
wrecks
marriages,
ruins
careers,
busts
reputations,
causes
heartaches,

nightmares,
indigestion,
spawns suspicion,
generates
grief,
dispatches
innocent
people
to cry in their
pillows.
Even its name
hisses.
It's called
gossip.
Office gossip.
Shop gossip.
Party gossip.
It makes
headlines
and headaches.
Before
you repeat
a story,
ask yourself:
Is it true?
Is it fair?
Is it necessary?
If not,
shut up.

Refraining from sin.   David describes the third mark of a person who would have intimacy with God as one "in whose eyes a reprobate is despised . . ." (Psalms 15:4).

This does not mean God encourages us to hate the reprobate, but we need to see his life in all its horror and commit ourselves to refraining from such a life-style. Reminding us that we live in a watching world, God calls us to a purity that says, "I can associate with the world for the purposes of glorifying my God, but for the good of my own soul, I must not be assimilated." Unless we can make that commitment to ourselves, the world will absorb us.

Walking among those who do not know Christ or claim to know Him but aren't living that way is a delicate and dangerous task:

> Thus says the Lord of hosts, Ask now the priests for a ruling: "If a man carries holy meat in the fold of his garment, and touches bread with this fold, or cooked food, wine, oil, or any other food, will it become holy?" And the priests answered and said, "No." Then Haggai said: "If one who is unclean from a corpse touches any of these, will the latter become unclean?" And the priests answered and said: "It will become unclean."
>
> Haggai 2:11

More often than not, that which is profane will desecrate that set aside for the purposes of God. Not only was that principle true in a pre-Christian community of faith, it also rings true in what often seems a post-Christian world. Whether or not we choose to admit it, the world influences us!

Several years ago, in the discussion that preceded the movie industry's introducing the rating of PG-13, *U.S. News and World Report* did a feature on the Motion Picture Association of America. It stated:

> Of 342 feature films classified by the Motion Picture Association of America last year, one was rated X—no one under 17 admitted. The R designation, meaning that no one under 17 is admitted unless accompanied by a parent, was given to 207 pictures. One-hundred-twenty-three movies were rated PG—parental guidance advised—and 11 were designated G, for general and unlimited admission. . . . In the past many movie makers resisted changing the system because some ratings markedly affect box-office receipts. G ratings are considered the kiss of death

for many films because teenagers often assume the movie won't be exciting. An X rating is equally unpalatable because film critics and advertising vehicles shy away from what is assumed to be a pornographic movie.

The G rating is a kiss of death, we are being told. In our world nobody wants to see a good squeaky-clean movie. Of course, we are not yet at the point where everyone rushes to see X-rated movies, but the film industry tries to group more and more in the middle. When they don't quite fit the way they'd like them to, they're even prepared to change the system! Movies showing some of the violence and teenage sex the industry would like to squeeze into this special category have become very popular:

> . . . [Dr. Thomas Radicky] a psychiatrist at the University of Illinois, says succeeding waves of movies, starting about 15 years ago, relied on more and more violence to attract crowds. Audiences became numbed to the repulsiveness of each level of violence they viewed, so directors had to enhance the horror in each new film to maintain interest. Violence has markedly increased since 1968 when the voluntary movie rating system started, says Radicky. He notes that 32 percent of movies released in 1969 were rated G, compared with a total of 4 percent in 1983. Radicky maintains that this spiral has become dangerous for children: "Kids get excited by gruesome brutality and they end up being criminals themselves."

If we don't keep ourselves from this world—whether we're talking about the movie industry or fads, the style of clothing or the materialism that attracts us all—it will suck us in and we'll become part of the system.

Recently I went shopping with my family at one of the most heavily trafficked malls in our land, where I was bombarded with sensory overload. The world does a good job of sending out its messages, communicating what it thinks we need . . . or quite honestly, what too often we *desire.* The eye gate takes it all in, as David knew so well when he reminded us that those who would know genuine intimacy with God can only be those "in whose eyes a reprobate is despised."

Sensitivity. Almost as if to contrast it with what has preceded, David continues by saying the one who enjoys genuine intimacy with God "honors those who fear the Lord." To become intimate with God, we must commit ourselves to purity, but we must also cultivate sensitivity toward others who fear the Lord.

As Proverbs 20:12 tells us, "The hearing ear and the seeing eye, The Lord has made both of them." God gave us ears with which we can hear the plaintive cries of those around us who hurt and know tremendous longings. With our eyes we may see the vacant stares of others, readily communicating emptiness, searching, and longing.

Within the household of faith many carry heavy burdens, and in them we see the truth of Solomon's words, "A plan in the heart of man is like deep water, But a man of understanding draws it out" (Proverbs 20:5). We need to look into the heart of another and know that he sails on troubled waters; then we need to help him come to grips with his pressing problems.

About three years ago I met with such understanding when I spoke at the annual conference for the Free Church Youth Fellowship of the Evangelical Free Church of America. Before I went into the auditorium, a youth pastor whom I had met several times before came up to me and said, "John, you look a bit troubled tonight. Let's pray together before you go in." I *was* troubled. About three months earlier I had made a decision that would affect my life, my ministry, and the lives of my wife and children. Suddenly, even though I had once believed the decision was God's will for me, I no longer felt comfortable with it. In fact, I knew I could not follow through. I lacked peace and had no idea how to extricate myself from an apparently irreversible situation. While I felt uncertain I had the courage to change, this young youth pastor came to me, saying, "You look troubled. Let me pray with you." When he put his arm around me and began to pray, I knew God would give me the courage . . . that I had made a bad decision . . . that it wasn't irreversible . . . and that when the time came to change it, just as God had brought along this near stranger to minister to me, those who loved me would not let go of me.

God gave us the seeing eye and hearing ear that we might become sensitive to one another, get caught up in one another's pain, and exercise the gifts He has given us, not only for His glory, but for the good of those in His family.

Consistency. Finally Psalms 15:4 ends by declaring that the one who would find closeness with God will be consistent: ". . . He swears to his own hurt, and does not change."

To develop consistency we must take on the nature of Christ, who is ". . . the same yesterday and today, yes and forever" (Hebrews 13:8). In an ever-changing world, we need to become as unchanging as He is.

Abraham counted on God's changelessness when it made no sense to believe. As he thought about his own body, as good as dead at a hundred years old, and when he thought about the deadness of Sarah's womb, Paul tells us the patriarch did not waver in unbelief, but grew strong in faith, giving glory to God. Abraham's life was marked with consistency: He held on to God and pressed toward what He had promised (Romans 4:19, 20).

Paul also reminds us that as we grow in Christ and approximate Him, we are no longer children, to be tossed here and there by waves and carried about by every wind of doctrine, trickery of man, or by craftiness and deceit (Ephesians 4:14).

Both passages speak of pressing on and the discipline that requires. Unless we make Him our chief desire and support that with the discipline of walking with Him, we cannot lay hold of God. Consistency doesn't just happen and doesn't come easily.

When I come home at the end of a day, I can pretty much tell where Rose had her coffee break. It's not that I see an empty coffee cup and napkin—I find her Bible there. From the very first she has treasured that Book as the love letter it really is. Because she delights in its pages and in disciplined study, God had given her a wonderful ministry to other women.

Rose's consistency has also enabled us to witness fruit in the lives of our children. When our oldest daughter came home from college on her first Christmas vacation, she said, "Let me share this Scripture with you," and recited the first two chapters of 1 Peter from memory. She was making this Scripture a deep part of her life. Every night, just after she sets her alarm, our middle daughter takes her devotional book and Bible and sets them open to her morning readings. Last Christmas our youngest daughter asked for only one gift—a devotional book, so she could have morning devotions. Though I'd like to tell you they've done all this because of my consistency, that would not be true. They learned it from Rose, who is so much more disciplined in her daily walk.

Over the years, in passing, I've been privileged to meet people who have achieved success, by the world's standards—actors and athletes who have made it to the top of their professions. But because we've been introduced, chatted a bit, and then moved on, they don't really know me, and I don't really know them. Somehow we've gotten the idea that just meeting God casually, the way I've met those men and women, is enough.

Through the prophet Jeremiah, God lets us know this is not so: "Let not a wise man boast of his wisdom, and let not the mighty man boast of his might, let not a rich man boast of his riches; but let him who boasts boast of this, that he understands and knows Me . . ." (9:23, 24). God wants us to know and experience intimacy that surpasses all the favors of the world, and we can never experience that in a short chat with Him.

Closeness with God begins with His acceptance and love of us, but it takes something on our part, too. We must have the right attitude and then appropriate that intimacy. Though we may know Him through nature, we will only see Him vaguely if we seek Him in a daily stroll through the countryside. We can know Him through trials, if we listen carefully; we meet Him in others if we look intently; and we can learn of Him through Scripture and prayer. But it also requires a disposition toward intimacy.

Appropriating Intimacy

What can we do to become intimate with God? Let's turn back to the Old Testament, to see how God met His people.

In Exodus 19 God called Moses and told him to prepare the Israelites for an encounter with Him. Verse 10 says God told Moses to assemble the people: "Go to the people and consecrate them today and tomorrow, and let them wash their garments; and let them be ready for the third day, for on the third day the Lord will come down from Mount Sinai in the sight of all the people." He's just told Moses to assemble more than 2 million people at the base of the mountain. Then He gives one restriction: "And you shall set bounds for the people all around, saying, 'Beware that you do not go up on the mountain or touch the border of it; whoever touches the mountain shall surely be put to death.' "

Why did God place this limitation on the people He called? Because He knew they were not determined to know Him. While Moses ascended the mountain with others, rather that determining to be right with God, the people played the whore. They danced and drank, fashioned a golden calf, and bent their knees to that idol.

Turn beyond that to Exodus 24, and you'll see God beckoning the elders of Israel to come up the mountain. "Then Moses went up with Aaron, Nadab and Abihu, and seventy of the elders of Israel" (v. 9). Of the 2 million, only a few elders went up to the mountain. "And they saw the God of Israel; and under His feet there appeared to be a pavement of sapphire, as clear as the sky itself. Yet He did not stretch out His hand against the nobles of the sons of Israel: and they beheld God, and they ate and drank"(vv. 10, 11). We often speak of knowing God, but have we ever seen Him? Those men did—but only two went on in the ascent that symbolized intimacy with God. Why? Because the others beheld God and ate and drank. They did not continue in His presence with awe and wonder; no permanent transformation occurred in their lives. Aaron will be found among the calf worshipers in Exodus 32. In Numbers 3:4 Nadab and Abihu die before the Lord because of their irreverence and disobedience. None of them had discipline.

"Now the Lord said to Moses, 'Come up to Me on the mountain and remain there, and I will give you the stone tablets with the law and the commandment which I have written for their instruction.' So Moses arose with Joshua his servant . . ." (Exodus 24:12, 13). They continue the climb. Why was Joshua different from the others? Why could he and Moses go up on the mountain, while the others had to stay below? The answer to that secret lies in Exodus 33, which tells us that Moses used to lead the people in worship. Whenever he went out to the tent of meeting, a cloud descended and stood at the entrance of the tent. The people watched, knowing God was speaking with Moses, and when he left the tent, the people went back to their own tents, and the experience had ended. While Moses was in the tent, the Lord spoke to him as a man speaks to his friend, face to face. However, when Moses returned to the camp, Joshua stayed there, because he was devoted; he knew God had been there. Joshua lingered where God had been.

Just as it did for Joshua, our intimacy with Him begins with a *determination* to lay hold of God. It continues with a *discipline* that keeps us from allowing life to return to business as usual after we've met Him. Finally it requires a *devotion*, a willingness to be where God is.

Even after all that, only one man continued all the way up the mountain. Exodus 24:16–18 tells us that the glory of the Lord rested on Mount Sinai; the cloud covered it for six days; and on the seventh He called to Moses from the midst of the cloud. To the sons of Israel, it looked like a consuming fire on the mountaintop, and Moses entered the cloud. The greatest leader of God's people knew genuine intimacy with Him. He heard the voice, and though he knew God's glory was like a consuming fire, he entered the cloud. Moses left everyone else behind him, because God called.

If we wish to know intimacy with the Master, we must be willing to step into His presence, even though we go alone. Knowing God does not happen in an instant. You can't signify it by raising your hand or walking down the aisle. It doesn't come from reciting a particular prayer or using a certain formula. Knowing God is the pursuit of a lifetime. We meet Him, and we learn Him. One day we'll meet Him face to face and will know Him even as we're known. Until then we pursue and seek to learn Him.

A. W. Tozer described those who are willing to commit their lives to laying hold of God this way:

> A real Christian is an odd number anyway. He feels supreme love for One whom he has never seen, talks familiarly every day to someone he cannot see, expects to go to heaven on the virtue of another, empties himself in order to be full, admits he's wrong so he can be declared right, goes down in order to get up, is strongest when he is weakest, richest when he is poorest, and happiest when he feels the worst. He dies so he can live, forsakes in order to have, gives away so he can keep, sees the invisible, hears the inaudible, and knows that which is beyond knowing.

That's really knowing God! As Christians we need to seek, pursue, and discipline ourselves as part of our regular spiritual life.

Two

Learning
to Love Him

I still recall the first time I met Ned and Margaret Thomas. . . .

Mom and Dad had invited Rose and me down from Vermont, to spend the weekend with them in their New York home. Why not? It sounded good to us. On Saturday afternoon, Mom told us she had invited a couple to join us for dessert that evening. Fine with us, we had no reason to give it a second thought.

Throughout that delightful weekend we *had* noticed Mom and Dad acted differently—especially Mom. She appeared happier than we had remembered her, and she talked about "the Lord." Her more than slight preoccupation with the Bible seemed rather unusual for us. As Catholics we were familiar with the Saint Joseph Missal and the Saint Andrew Missal, but we hadn't spent a great deal of time—if any—studying the Bible. In fact, I'm not sure I could have told you where to find a Bible in our Vermont home—if we even had one!

As the guests arrived that evening, I immediately spotted the gilt-edged black Bibles tucked under their arms. I knew then that this was no casual dessert: This was a calculated evening—a spiritual ambush!

Conversation began casually enough. The Thomases carefully directed the conversation back to Rose and myself—who we were . . . where our interests lay . . . what our hope and aspirations for life were.

Mom called us to the table for dessert. I had looked forward to that. . . . As we came to the table, Mom looked at Ned and asked, "Would you please say grace?"

That's a bit much, I thought. *We just said grace with dinner, a little over two hours ago.* I had spoken the prayer we'd used for years—wasn't it effective anymore? Besides, we never prayed over dessert. But Ned bowed and prayed—especially for Rose and me.

As we began to eat, Ned remarked that he understood I had studied almost nine years for the priesthood. That led to a discussion of monasticism and the Catholic Church. They were very good listeners. The Thomases hadn't come to do all the talking. Then—a bit later—they began to speak about Jesus. . . .

Often I've looked back at that night and wondered just what enabled Ned and Margaret Thomas to bring me to that place of decision. The tool was incidental, their technique immaterial, but the overall method was most effective. How did they ever get an ex-monk, a member of the parish council and teacher of the Senior High Confraternity of Christine Doctrine Class to the place of saying yes to Christ?

When Ned asked me if I knew Jesus, I almost laughed. *Did I know Jesus?* For nine years I had studied to be an *alter Christus,* "another Christ"—a priest, and *he* wanted to know if *I* knew Jesus?

But before long I realized Ned and his wife had something I did not have—and I desperately needed and wanted that something. I owned religion, but they offered reality. It shone through their very lives. I didn't want to admit it. In fact I treated them harshly at first, but they held up under my abuse and scrutiny.

Nicodemus told Jesus, "Rabbi, we know that You have come from God as a teacher; for no one can do these signs that You do unless God is with him" (John 3:2). I, too, understood that no one could live, speak, and love the way this couple did unless they had the genuine article— the Living Christ. If He could live within them, I wanted Him to live in me. Their lives drew me like a magnet, but their love for Jesus was the method they used to share Him.

Commission or Commandment?

As evangelicals bent on reaching the world for Christ, most of us have come to regard evangelism as our objective. Deliberately we have made the Final Commission of Christ first and foremost—but the Master never intended that. He saw evangelism—the fulfillment of the Final Commission—as a by-product, not the ultimate goal. He said, "Go therefore and make disciples of all the nations, baptizing them in the name of the Father and the Son and the Holy Spirit, teaching them to observe all that I commanded you; and lo, I am with you always, even to the end of the age (Matthew 28:19, 20).

We have taken as our banner "go therefore and make disciples of all the nations," but the Greek text actually reads "as you go." In other words, evangelism should flow from our daily lives. It should take place between Sundays as we seek to fulfill the First and Foremost Commandment, not the Final Commission.

The First and Foremost Commandment has to do with radical commitment. We find it in the twelfth chapter of the Gospel of Mark, where Jesus answers the question of a young scribe. In talking to the Sadducees, Pharisees, and scribes, Jesus found Himself in the middle of a theological firing squad. They asked about an explosive issue—resurrection. On the surface, the discussion seems to be about the idea of marriage as an eternal bond. In reality the Sadducees wanted Jesus to deny the resurrection, siding with them against the Pharisees.

One scribe, greatly impressed with Jesus' answer to that question, dared to ask the Master a question that weighed heavy on his heart: "What commandment is the foremost of all?" (v. 28). Jesus' answer was not unknown to that scribe, for He quoted the Great Shema, the daily prayer of the devout Jew: "Hear, O Israel! the Lord our God is one Lord; and you shall love the Lord your God with all your heart, and with all your soul, and with all your mind, and with all your strength" (vv. 29, 30).

Not only is this the First and Foremost Commandment, it also succinctly states the Master's concept of discipleship. For Jesus, commitment is truly radical, going to the root of our beings. This mandate, which addresses the things we love, recognizes our proper starting point in reaching the world for Christ.

Reaching Out With Love

In this commandment, Jesus speaks of a love so complete that it embraces all we are, our hearts, souls, minds, and strength. So compelling is the love that it ought to empty the pews of our churches and send us out into the streets of the world. So convincing is this love of God it entices others to say, "I want what you have. . . . I need what you've got."

The Latin adage *Nemo dat quod non habet*, "No one gives what he does not have," states a simple truth. Stop and try to recall when someone last approached you and demanded, "Give me what you have." If love for Christ doesn't shine through as it ought, people may not come and say, "Give me." Even if they do, sometimes we're not quite sure what to give.

How Do I Love Thee?

". . . Love the Lord your God . . . ," commands Jesus, but we may love in several ways.

A. W. Tozer tells us there's a love that springs from appreciation. The Psalmist expresses this when he sings: "I love the Lord because He hears My voice and my supplications" (Psalms 116:1). John reminds us, "We love, because He first loved us" (1 John 4:19). Such gratitude is rational love, and we give it because God has done something for us.

In Solomon's Song of Songs, when the young woman describes the object of her love: "My beloved is dazzling and ruddy, Outstanding among ten thousand," she shows love that stems from appreciation. Awakened and nurtured by seeing excellence, grace, or beauty, such love seems a bit more elevated than the first kind, because selfishness is somewhat reduced.

Both kinds of love share a common element: They are rational. Each points to a reason for their existence.

A third type—suprarational love—goes beyond these. On the purely human level, Steve and Judy have such love for their third child.

Just before they adopted this little guy—blind, mute, unable to walk or do for himself and pretty much unwanted and unloved—the neurologist met with them to remind them this baby would never be more than a rag doll. He would never care for himself . . . nor would he express any gratitude for their saving his life and committing themselves to serving and caring for him.

They took the child anyway and named him *Christopher,* "Christ bearer." And they love him as fully as their own two, normal children. Suprarational love like theirs is wonderful to see. Not "I love because," but simply, "I love."

In the First and Foremost Commandment Jesus speaks not only of love of appreciation or admiration. His command stands stark naked, apart from reason: "Love the Lord your God." Certainly it will include a love of gratitude and an appreciation of His Person will awaken and nurture it. But the love He describes must also exist apart from what He's done. It embraces the four areas involved in a radical commitment: heart . . . soul . . . mind . . . and strength.

Fourfold Love

What does loving God this way require of us? It comes. . . .

From the Center of Human Affection

". . . Love the Lord your God with all you heart . . . ," Jesus continued His commandment, referring to the center of all human affection, which we must turn totally on God. "If anyone comes to Me, and does not hate his own father and mother and wife and children and brothers and sisters, yes, and even his own life, he cannot be My disciple," proclaimed our Lord (Luke 14:26).

We all know He was not speaking of an absolute hate— but that in comparison to the love He requires for discipleship, all other loves must be lesser. Not only must they pale into insignificance, in contrast they might even seem like hate. Simply put, Jesus demands unrivaled love— unrivaled by family ties or by fondness for this world's goods.

What of love that does not meet His standard? James the brother of Jesus warns us ". . . Do you not know that friendship with the world is hostility toward God? . . ." (4:4). Sören Kierkegaard spoke of the same thing when he saw commitment as a wholehearted decision: "A person cannot by the craft and flattery of tongue lay hold of God while his heart is far away."

The prophet Isaiah spoke for God, explaining His disappointment in His people: "Because this people draw near with their words And honor Me with their lip service, But they remove their hearts far from Me, And their reverence for Me consists of tradition learned by rote" (29:13). He demands a wholehearted commitment, centered on Him.

Several years ago, my wife and I shared some thoughts we had gleaned from the writings of Ann Kiemel, whose depth of commitment and sincere love for the Savior have blessed us. At one point Rose looked at me and asked, "Do you know that kind of intimacy with the Master? Do you have that kind of relationship with Jesus?"

"No," I replied. "I really don't, Rose. I work for Him. I know I love Him. I would not work as I do for any earthly concern. I believe my work is all for Him. But I've become so busy about the work that I've neglected the heart of the relationship . . . I've neglected the intimacy."

In His commandment Jesus is speaking of that kind of heart relationship. He will brook no rivals in intimacy, even if it involves our work for Him. Never confuse involvement in ministry with intimacy with the Master.

From the Center of Human Motivation

Jesus continued the commandment, "And love the Lord your God . . . with all your soul." When we use the word *soul*, for the most part we refer to the essence of personhood, that within us created in the image and likeness of God, making us capable of a unique relationship with Him. Not only must we love God from the center of our human affection, we must love Him from our soul, the center of human motivation.

Recently a *New York Times* writer shouted through her articles, "I want life—not a lifestyle." That's the idea here. Jesus does not merely want us to express our love for God by adherence to a life-style—not even a conservative evangelical one, whatever that might be.

Instead love for Christ should cause us to live from the inside out. As we love God with all our souls, we experience the thirsting described in Psalms 63:1, 8: "O, God, Thou art my God; I shall seek Thee earnestly; My soul thirsts for Thee . . . in a dry and weary land where there is no water . . . My soul clings to Thee." As David's soul follows fast in pursuit of God, his heart cries out from the center of his being.

In *The Last Crusade*, Major V. Gilbert describes the thirst he and his men suffered in the Palestinian desert during World War I:

> Our heads ached. Our eyes became bloodshot and dim in the blinding glare . . . Our tongues began to swell . . . our lips turned to purplish black and burst. Those who dropped out of the column were never seen again, but the desperate force battled on to Sheria. There were wells at

Sheria, and had they been unable to take the place by nightfall, thousands were doomed to die of thirst. We fought that day as men fight for their lives. We entered Sheria's station on the heels of the retreating Turks. The first objects which met our view were the great stone cisterns full of cold, clear drinking water. . . . It took four hours before the last man had his drink of water. . . . I believe that we all learned our first Bible lesson on that march from Beersheba to the Sheria wells. If such were our thirst for God and for righteousness, for His Will in our lives, a consuming, all-embracing, preoccupying desire, how rich in the fruit of the Spirit would we be.

How many of us have experienced such thirst for our God? At the place where decisions are made, do we desire Him? Can we say we love Him with all our souls—a consuming, all-embracing, preoccupying desire for His Person and the glory of His purposes? Do we love God from the inside out?

From the Center of Human Cognition

"Love the Lord your God . . . with all your mind." Too many of us think this means merely giving intellectual assent to all the truths of the gospel, but loving God mentally means far more than that. To actually love Him in the center of human cognition, we have to exercise our whole minds. By daring to ask ourselves hard questions and not remaining content with sing-song answers that are little more than cliches, we can spend our energies, our life strength, in study of them.

A dear friend and learned scientist, Dr. Ken Radimer, once said to me, "John, for too long fundamentalists have consigned any thinking, questioning mind to hell. Without losing the gift of love in the process, we need to regain this world's recognition that one of the Lord's gifts is that of a sound mind." How sad that though we may possess the truth, we have become intellectually dishonest.

Too often we just become too mentally lazy, and our

lethargy in our pursuit of God is reflected in our slow-footed pursuit of a lost people.

Only by committing our minds to the pursuit of God can we truly know Him. Meeting Him is not enough; we need to *know* Him. "Why did God make me?" asks the Baltimore catechism. And it answers, "God made me to know Him, to love Him, and to serve Him in this life that I might be happy with Him in the next." No greater challenge to the mind exists than knowing his ways . . . His works . . . His words . . . the wonder of His Person!

Just months—possibly weeks—before dying for his faith, Paul wrote his young disciple Timothy, pleading, ". . . When you come bring the cloak which I left at Troas with Carpus, and the books, especially the parchments" (2 Timothy 4:13). Confined in the dank, dark Mamertine Prison, at the onset of winter, the apostle wanted a warm cloak, but even more he wanted his books and parchments—quite possibly the letters he was writing. Facing imminent death, he continued using his mind in pursuit of the One he met on the Damascus Road.

Fifteen centuries later, from the Vilvorde Prison in Belgium, William Tyndale wrote the governor:

> I entreat your lordship, and that by the Lord Jesus, that if I must remain here for the winter you would beg the Commissary to be so kind as to send me, from the things of mine which he has, a warmer cap; I feel the cold painfully in my head. Also a warmer cloak, for the cloak I have is very thin. He has a woollen shirt of mine, if he will send it. But most of all, my Hebrew Bible, Grammar and Vocabulary, that I may spend my time in that pursuit.

Shortly afterwards, he, too, would become a martyr for his faith.

How many of us have the discipline of an uncluttered mind—stretching ourselves in study, prayer, and praise, despite circumstances?

When Paul came to Thessalonica, he went to "a synagogue of the Jews. And according to Paul's custom, he went to them, and for three Sabbaths reasoned with them from the Scriptures, explaining and giving evidence that the Christ had to suffer and rise again from the dead, and saying, 'This Jesus whom I am proclaiming to you is the Christ' " (Acts 17:1–3). Did you catch that? Witnessing to the Jews was his custom—no silent witness here. Paul provoked thought among his listeners: He reasoned . . . he explained . . . he gave evidence.

Truly faith alone saves, but isn't it time the lost heard a clear, ordered, logical apologetic for the Person and work of Jesus Christ? Our faith need not do violence to our intelligence; we need not only speak about experience. When he appealed to the Jewish populace, in Acts 22, Paul spoke of personal experience, but he also offered evidence. As he spoke of Jesus the Nazarene a hush fell over the audience, who fully understood he spoke of a Man who was crucified, dead, and buried. By proclaiming he had met Him on the Damascus Road, Paul boldly affirmed Jesus' death and resurrection.

When we use our minds to explain the gospel, let's be careful of the stories we silently receive or solemnly repeat. We need not resort to attacks on religions, denominations, or persons.

Not long ago I spoke at a banquet, and in his introduction the master of ceremonies alluded to my time in the monastery. The next morning a man approached me and told me he, too, had spent many years in a religious order. Though I had already heard of him, I wanted to see if this man dared tell me the same tales he had told others. He claimed to have been a Jesuit who studied with the order from age twelve, until he left them at forty. Before long I knew he told others the old hate stories I had heard soon after my conversion.

This man told his ready audience that the Jesuits were out to get him; his car had been firebombed twice; and from time to time someone would approach him, saying, "We know where you are." He spared me those stories, but I still felt compelled to find out more about his background. When was he ordained priest? I asked. Just how old was he at the time of his ordination? Without blinking an eye, he responded, "I was eighteen."

"No, no. Not how old you were when you professed vows, but how old were you when you were ordained?"

Again he answered, "Eighteen."

The simple truth is that nobody is now, or ever has been, ordained priest in the Catholic Church at eighteen. Canon law *mandates* that a man be at least twenty-four. There can be no waiver of that requirement.

While certain groups may love to hear such stories, and the speaker who tells them will never lack an audience, they are just not true.

We cannot participate in that kind of ministry, because it is not ministry, but an abuse of the minds God gave us for pursuit and proclamation of the truth. He calls us to love Him with all our minds. Let's use them for His glory. The gospel is too positive to allow us to indulge in negatives. It is a story of love; we need not and ought not speak things that make for hate.

From the Center of Human Volition

"And you shall love the Lord your God with all your heart, and with all your soul, and with all your mind, and with all your strength." Tough order, "all your strength." To me this means loving God with all you've got, 100 percent for Him.

We've already seen that God must be the center of human affection, human motivation, and human cognition. Now He has to be the center of human volition. We need to love Him where our will exercises its prerogatives.

Other places in the Scriptures refer to this idea, too. Solomon challenges us, "Whatever your hand finds to do, verily do it with all your might . . ." (Ecclesiastes 9:10). Writing his first letter to the church at Corinth, Paul describes this full-throttle living, "But by the grace of God I am what I am, and His grace toward me did not prove vain; but I labored [in the Greek this word conveys "to the very point of exhaustion"] even more than all of them, yet not I, but the grace of God with me" (15:10).

Ex-communist Douglas Hyde offers insight that causes us to reexamine our ideas of commitment:

> If you ask me what is the distinguishing mark of the Communist . . . what it is that Communists have most outstandingly in common, I would not say, as some people expect, their ability to hate—this is by no means common to them all. I would say that, beyond any shadow of doubt, it is their idealism . . . their zeal . . . their dedication . . . devotion to their cause . . . and their willingness to sacrifice. This is no accident. It does not just happen. If the majority of members of any organization are half-hearted and largely inactive, then it is not surprising if others who join it soon conform to that same general pattern. If the organization makes relatively few demands upon its members, and if they quite obviously feel under no obligation to give a great deal to it, then those who join may be forgiven for supposing that this is the norm and that this is what membership entails. The Communists make far bigger demands upon their people than the average Christian organization would ever dare to make. They believe that if you make big demands on people you will get a big response. So this is made a deliberate policy on their part. They never make a small demand if they can make the big one.

Christ has made a big demand of us in this First and Foremost Commandment. When He asks that we love God with all our strength, He issues a call to excellence. Too long has the twentieth-century world been deprived of seeing all the church could be and do, if only its members would commit themselves to full-throttle living . . . each running the race with his or her best.

Vince Lombardi spoke of this type of excellence:

> I owe most everything to football, in which I have spent the greater part of my life. And I have never lost my respect for what I consider a great game. And each Sunday, after the battle, one group savors victory, another group

lives in the bitterness of defeat. The many hurts seem a
small price to have paid for having won, and there is no
reason at all that is adequate for having lost. To the winner
there is one hundred percent elation, one hundred percent
laughter, one hundred percent fun; and to the loser the
only thing left for him is a one hundred percent resolution,
one hundred percent determination. And it's a game, I
think, a great deal like life in that it demands that a man's
personal commitment be toward excellence and be toward
victory, even though you know that ultimate victory can
never be completely won. Yet it must be pursued with all
one's might. And each week there's a new encounter, each
year a new challenge. But all of the rings and all of the
money and all of the color and all of the display, they
linger only in the memory. The spirit, the will to win, and
the will to excel, these are the things that endure and these
are the qualities that are much more important than any of
the events that occasion them. And I'd like to say that the
quality of a man's life has got to be a full measure of that
man's personal commitment to excellence and to victory,
regardless of what field he may be in.

Should we give less to Jesus than Lombardi's players gave
him? As children of the heavenly Father, we should make
a life of love for, and loyalty to, the Master our mark.

One saint said: "We should not see ourselves so much
living in the world and bearing witness to Christ as living
in Christ and bearing witness to the world." Such a witness
screams far more loudly than any silent witness, tract,
religious survey, or street-corner meeting ever could. It's
not routine . . . it's not ritual . . . and it's not religion! I
didn't see any of those things in Ned and Margaret Thomas.
I saw the reality of Jesus . . . because they *loved* Him!

The *All* of the Early Church

If we look at the Book of Acts, we can see how this full
commitment to Christ was evidenced in the early church.

Acts 4 tells us of Barnabas, who sold a tract of land
and gave *all* the proceeds to the community of faith. His

action seemed to make no sense—except that nothing rivaled his love for God. Of the rest of that church, the Spirit of God prompted Luke to say: "And day by day continuing with one mind in the temple, and breaking bread from house to house, they were taking their meals together with gladness and sincerity of heart, praising God, and having favor with all the people. And the Lord was adding to their number day by day those who were being saved" (Acts 2:46, 47). The Lord Jesus was in the center of their hearts.

The life of Stephen shows us more than 100 percent living. Despite the fact that an angry mob rejected his presentation of Christ, stoning him, he called on the Lord, "Lord Jesus, receive my spirit! And falling on his knees, he cried out with a loud voice, 'Lord do not hold this sin against them!' And having said this, he fell asleep" (Acts 7:59, 60). Right to the end, Stephen lived what he believed.

The fruit of Stephen's life is evidenced in the changed life of a man who held others' robes while they stoned Stephen. Saul of Tarsus—later the apostle Paul—would never forget Stephen's steadfastness.

Acts 11:19 tells us of the scattering of the faithful ". . . because of the persecution that arose in connection with Stephen. . . ." Believers made their way to Phoenicia, Cyprus, and Antioch, and the text makes it clear that in Antioch many believed, and their changed lives evidenced God's grace. Because this new life shone from within, at Antioch the believers were first called "Christ ones"—*Christians*.

Tracing Paul's path, we find clusters of believers standing firm for Christ in their newfound faith. His farewell at Ephesus speaks of that commitment in his life: "But I do not consider my life of any account as dear to myself, in order that I may finish my course, and the ministry which I received from the Lord Jesus, to testify solemnly of the gospel of the grace of God" (Acts 20:24). Paul did not consider life too dear. He would spend his energies, willing to finish the course for Christ.

A New Commitment

In our own lives we have to make a new commitment to the Final Commission. But any attempt to do that before we come to grips with the First and Foremost Commandment will not ring true. Before speaking of His love for the world, we must love him fully, with heart, soul, mind, and strength.

Some of my close friends chide me from time to time that I remain more than just a bit Catholic. Freely I admit some things carry over in my life and ministry. Among them, the crucifix remains dear to me.

Now, I know Christ is no longer dead, that He was taken down from the cross, laid in the tomb, and rose from the grave. But every once in a while, possibly because of my time spent with the Passionists—good men who dearly loved the Lord Jesus and spent their time reflecting on His sorrows and sufferings—from time to time I take my old crucifix and hold it in my hands. It serves as a powerfully vivid reminder of all He suffered, how He was beaten, nailed to that tree, then bled and died for me. At moments like that, when I think of His great love, I become reflective and question my love in terms of my heart, because Jesus said, "John, where your treasure is, there will your heart be also." Studying the crucifix, I ask, *Where do my affections center?*

Next I question my motivation, because life has to be lived from the inside out. Especially in ministry, at times I must ask, *Why am I doing this?* Then Paul's words come back to me: "And whatever you do in word or deed, do all in the name of the Lord Jesus, giving thanks through Him to God the Father" (Colossians 3:17).

Like other men, I also struggle with my mind; with ease it wanders and gives itself over to idleness. Again the words of the apostle challenge me: "Set your mind on the things above . . ." (Colossians 3:2). So I ask, *Am I really exercising my mind by time spent in His Word? Do I seek opportunities to learn more about Jesus?* Then I must ask myself about my mind's processes: Am I striving, as Paul challenged, to think on whatever is true and honorable, right and pure, lovely, of good repute? Have I committed and submitted my mind to the lordship of Jesus?

Finally the crucifix compels me to examine the matter of volition: *Am I striving to live for Him, putting all my energies into accomplishing His will?* Jesus Himself set the standard, "If anyone loves Me, he will keep My word. . . . He who does not love Me does not keep My words. . . ." At times I ask myself if the things to which I give my strength truly evidence a willed love for Him. The crucifix causes my heart to want to sing:

> *My Jesus, I love Thee, I know Thou art mine—*
> *For Thee all the follies of sin I resign;*
> *My gracious Redeemer, my Savior art Thou.*
> *If ever I loved Thee, my Jesus, 'tis now.*
>
> WILLIAM R. FEATHERSTON

But I want that to be more than a song. I desire it to be my life. . . .

Three

Serving Without _____ *Mixed Motives*

Two days in my life stand out in stark contrast. On the first day, in late fall, 1967, I remember driving along Skunk Hallow Road in a November snowfall. Only out of the army a few months, I still missed it terribly, despite the good job I had teaching at Woodstock Union High School. Caught in an oppressive conflict, I struggled with feelings of guilt over some of the things I had done as an army intelligence agent . . . my life had no true meaning or direction . . . many people saw me as an angry young man, mad at the world, ready to do battle over anything . . . I seriously questioned the value of continuing life.

As the snow fell, I reached up, in a rather dramatic moment, and shut off my Bronco's windshield wipers. Almost instantly snow covered the windshield. I immediately put them back on, but those few seconds stand out in my mind as a time when I really didn't want to live. Only the thought of Rose and our first baby, Laura Lynn, made me realize I had a great deal to live for. But my depression continued. . . .

The following March Rose and I met Christ. Sixteen

months beyond that, my life had changed radically. Driving along Nesconset Highway, the top of my convertible down, the sun beating down on me, I felt very much alive. Now that I appreciated the pardon of Christ as Lord, I no longer labored under the guilt of past mistakes. I had a genuine purpose in life: I wanted to glorify God. Peace with the world, my family, my siblings (who seemed to have accomplished more than I) all stemmed from my peace with God. New power from Him enabled me to get up each morning and believe my life counted for God and the people with whom I came in touch.

Continuing down the highway, a thought returned to me—one I had frequently tried to banish from my mind. As often as I'd try to block it out, the same idea returned to me, now with more force than ever. I came to a traffic light. Turning right would take me home; left went toward the parsonage. I made the left, on the chance that Pastor Tapper might be home; turning into the driveway, I saw him and his family in the backyard.

Kindly, Bob Tapper pulled himself away from his family when I asked to speak to him. Blurting out my confusion, I told him, "Pastor, I don't even know how to begin. But this thought has haunted me so much lately . . . I place absolutely no value in it . . . I've tried over and over to dismiss it from my mind. But I need your help: I've struggled with the thought of entering the ministry." A warm smile crossed his face, almost announcing that God had just answered one of his prayers. We talked a while, agreeing on an action plan that would help me ascertain God's will for my life.

When I went home and shared all this with Rose, she spoke words of encouragement and confirmation: "Lately, John, I've been reflecting on how greatly God has changed our lives, how different things have been in these last months since we've accepted Christ. I, too, have thought how wonderful it would be if we could begin to tell others about Christ."

So began a chain of events that led me to study for the ministry and work within the Evangelical Free Church of

America. But even early on, I had to wrestle with *why?* *Why ministry?* The question haunted me, and the answer was important.

Already I'd started down that track in the Catholic Church, with the Passionist Fathers. But I'd realized that road was not for me. Why now did I feel this urgency to enter the ministry? Before I even thought of uprooting my young family, I wanted to be sure. I needed to know *why* I should enter such service.

Checking Our Motives

Since that time, I've come to realize that whenever we mention motives, we walk on sacred ground. I've delighted in asking people *why* they do the things they do. . . .

A few years ago, my friend Tom, a very successful young restaurateur, began to give me the feeling he had taken his eyes off Christ, in the rush of making his business successful. Even at the end of the day Tom focused his thoughts on the morrow and all he had yet to accomplish.

"Tom," I asked. "What motivates you and keeps you going?"

"The race, John. I have to keep the bills paid and stay ahead of it."

But as Tom's success increased, his excitement for Christ and His church seemed to wane.

In contrast, an older woman, Maria has raised her children and ended a successful career as a middle manager. On the go from morning to night, as part of the ministry staff at a large Christian conference center, she cares for people older than herself.

"Who winds you up?" I questioned. "Why all this investment of time in older people?"

Without hesitation, she responded, "People. I love people. And I want them to see the love of Jesus in me. It's all just a platform from which I can say, 'God loves you!' "

Why we do the things we do is what motivation is all about. Webster defines *motive* as "an emotion or a desire operating on the will and causing one to act."

Motive is not just an inner movement—it is an inner movement that impacts our wills and causes us to act. Motives move us to do. Desire makes us willingly do something, despite the obstacles before us. No longer do we have to be prodded, if we have desire. We keep on going because our task or goal has become a joy to us or because it will profit us.

We cannot always judge the motives of others, but we must not fail to examine our own. Self-scrutiny helps us determine if we are in fact serving *ourselves* or God.

Too easily can we fall prey to the standards and values of this world. Jeremiah warns, "The heart is the most deceitful thing there is, and desperately wicked. No one can really know how bad it is! Only the Lord knows! He searches all hearts and examines deepest motives so He can give to each person his right reward . . ." (17:9, 10 TLB). As we make His Word a part of our self-examination we will see clearly to judge ourselves. If our motives become clouded with sin, He cannot bless them, and inappropriate motives can neutralize a Christian's impact on the world.

Why do you want to serve? Are you centered on Him?

Missing Your Serve

In his study on motivation, *Be a Leader People Follow*, David L. Hocking presents some attitudes that can interfere with our service for Christ. From his work I've drawn five motives we as Christians must root up from our lives if we wish to serve Him.

Pride

Some people serve because they want to be first. Such folks concern themselves with lofty titles and fancy offices, but remain blind to the needs of those around them. Bent on adding to their own authority, they fail to serve others.

The Master made it very clear that doesn't work in His church:

. . . You know that those who are recognized as rulers of the Gentiles lord it over them; and their great men exercise authority over them. But it is not so among you, but whoever wishes to become great among you shall be your servant; and whoever wishes to be first among you shall be slave of all. For even the Son of Man did not come to be served, but to serve, and to give His life a ransom for many.

Mark 10:42–45

The best leader has no haughty spirit, but a servant's heart. The life of a Spirit-filled believer holds no room for the tendency to dominate and control others.

The proud person feels a sense of satisfaction in dominating others, failing to recognize the importance and dignity of each individual. You've seen such leaders in the church, and so did the apostles. In his third letter John tells of a man who was not very docile and longed to teach others before anyone else could teach him. He writes, ". . . Diotrephes, who loves to be first among them, does not accept what we say"(v.9). Because he had to be first, he refused to submit to John's leadership.

The Book of Revelation may show that the Nicolaitans shared this failing. To the church at Ephesus Jesus said, ". . . You hate the deeds of the Nicolaitans, which I also hate" (2:6). Though He never told us exactly what He hated in their deeds, their name may provide a clue: *Nikao* is a Greek verb that means "to conquer or vanquish"; *laos* means "people." Perhaps they had fallen into the sin of dominating others, because of their pride. If so, theirs was no fit motive for ministry.

Deep down in our hearts, we know we are all prone to pride and it destroys ministry. Solomon's words, "A man's pride will bring him low . . ." hit home; however, he also prescribes the antidote, ". . . But a humble spirit will obtain honor" (Proverbs 29:23). As we seek humility in our service, we may also discover some unexpected benefits!

Prestige

Our own press clippings always look good to us—but we have to be on guard that we don't become overly impressed with our own achievements.

Have you ever met a man or woman in Christian circles who became preoccupied with a long list of honors bestowed on him or her? Jane B. Christian may become preoccupied with all her proper introductions and her well-known friends. James Q. Christian may focus on a long list of honorary degrees and his full-blown resume. They've lost focus on the life of faith.

John the Baptist affords the best example of how a Christian needs to live. Impressed with the man, Jewish leaders sent priests and Levites to meet this wild prophet with strange clothes and a weird diet. They wanted to know who he was . . . or at least who he thought he was. John clearly told them he was only a man, not God . . . he was the sent one, not the Sender . . . a lamp, not the Light. The Baptist never paused to wonder if the crowds confirmed the effectiveness of his ministry, because he knew he prepared the way for the One to follow—the One whose sandal he felt unworthy to untie!

When John said, "He must increase . . . I must decrease" (John 3:30), he summed up his life message and ministry as well as his view of prestige.

On the day I was ordained, a group of men stood around me as I knelt and, each with a hand on my shoulder, asked a blessing. My father, as part of that service, prayed an eloquently simple prayer: "Father, for this one called John I ask only that his life's prayer be that of another named John—that Jesus increase . . . and he decrease." When I think of his prayer, the words of God, spoken through Jeremiah, come to mind: ". . . Let not a wise man boast of his wisdom, and let not the mighty man boast of his might, let not a rich man boast of his riches; but let him who boasts boast of this, that he understands and knows Me, that I am the Lord who exercises lovingkindness, justice, and righteousness on earth; for I delight in these things . . ." (9:23, 24). Both show a right perception of the world!

When we come to the bottom line, we should be like the title of a book by Allan C. Emery: *A Turtle on a Fencepost.* When you see a turtle there, you know he never climbed up on his own—someone put him there! In the same way, a man elevated to prominence and a position of high visibility must remember that God placed him there. Despite what he says and what others might like to believe, he did not get there on his own merits and ability.

The antidote for our desire for prestige is learning to say no to our propensity for saying yes to self. When we become proud of our accomplishments, we need to remember the words of Solomon: "Let another praise you, and not your own mouth; A stranger, and not your own lips" (Proverbs 27:2).

Personal Needs

Most of us in people-oriented professions have real people needs ourselves. As we long for appreciation, affection, and affirmation, if we give ourselves to meeting those needs in the lives of others, we find our own needs met.

In meeting the needs of others, we are given a certain amount of power over them. Dr. Paul Tournier acknowledged that when he said that physicians like himself have chosen "a vocation of power." Placed in an arena where technical skill and knowledge accentuate the dependency of others on him, the doctor can feel superior. Tournier concluded, "To be looked upon as a Savior leaves none of us indifferent."

The same thing happens with those in ministry to others, he observed. We need to remain aware of the temptation to control, manipulate, and exploit those we seek to "help." Giving a hand to people who have experienced real stress and confusion in their lives means we play an ego-satisfying and powerful role. Whether or not we consciously realize it, that involves an element of domination and desire to increase our own power. As Tournier says, "There is in us especially in those whose intentions are the purest, an excessive and destructive need for power which eludes even the most sincere and honest self-examination."

Those of us who minister must honestly face the possibility that caring stems from the appreciation, affection, and affirmation we expect in return. Or it may be rooted in a wish to control—basing all leadership on authority and a sense of power.

Instead the ministering Christian must, as Hocking points out, have childlike trust. God knows all our needs and has promised to meet them. As the shepherd-king said, "The Lord is my Shepherd. I have everything that I need" (*see* Psalms 23:1). Peter described real trust as "casting all your anxiety upon Him, because He cares for you"(1 Peter 5:7).

In addition, every leader must be committed to self-scrutiny. Since we easily fall prey to deception, we need to examine our actions in the light of God's Word, which is ". . . living and active and sharper than any two-edged sword, piercing as far as the division of soul and spirit, of both joints and marrow, and able to judge the thoughts and intentions of the heart" (Hebrews 4:12).

Propriety

When we do things out of a sense of oughtness, rendering a perfunctory performance because others expect or demand it of us, we slide into the pitfall of propriety.

God has given us each definite gifts, to use in the local church, for the common good. Therefore, I believe anyone who is not gifted for a particular ministry but does it anyway is outside the will of God. Not to use our gifts diminishes His glory and deprives the church—and that is sin.

Though we may hear much about spiritual gifts, rarely will we hear about using them with balance; yet if we don't use them wisely, we cannot have effective ministries. Many good, concerned people feel that every call from the pulpit and every mention of a need for workers is aimed at them. Because they long to see their church known as a loving and caring assembly of Christians, they earnestly long to see every vacuum filled—even at their own expense.

As a result, pastoral staffs turn to such individuals far too often. Over and over again they ask the same body of workers to take on the tasks, until those few have lost all joy in ministry. What they once did with spontaneous enthusiasm has become an obligation. As first-love excitement dies a sense of guilt for feeling a rising resentment replaces it. Ultimately the people with needs do not have them met, because the workers have become overtaxed. If any pitfall to ministry seems understandable, it is this one. Even though those who fall into the propriety trap have the best of motives, we have to control the inroads it can make on a ministry. Overwork consumes the energies of the conscientious and stunts spiritual growth.

A two-fold antidote does exist. First we need to understand that ". . . where the Spirit of the Lord is, there is liberty" (2 Corinthians 3:17) and enjoy that liberty. Accept the Spirit-given freedom of choosing where to serve, and use the gifts He has given you. Know, too, that as you walk in that liberty, "There is . . . no condemnation for those who are in Christ Jesus" (Romans 8:1).

If you struggle with serving God from a sense of oughtness, you have taken too much on yourself. If you wear two, three, or four hats in the assembly, for your own sake, shed your guilt. Don't let another person write the script for your life. Free yourself from too many burdens and enjoy *a* ministry.

Popular Acclaim

Finally, we may seek to serve for the applause of men. However, such seeking for popular acclaim has a great deal to do with buying into the world's system: We've succumbed to the success syndrome of our century.

Whether or not we choose to admit it, the struggle for success has caught most of us, to the point where we expect others to buy in, too. Chuck Swindoll masterfully points out the prevalence of this problem:

> When you stop achieving long enough to think about it, our world is full of overexpecters. They are in every profession, most of the schools, many of the shops, and (dare I say it?) all the churches.

To the overexpecter, enough is never enough. There's always room for improvement, always an area or two that isn't quite up to snuff, always something to criticize. Always. The overexpecter uses words like "ought" and "should" and loves sentences that include "must" and "more." To them, "work harder" and "move faster" and "do better" and "reach higher" are the rule rather than the exception. When you're around them you get the distinct impression that no matter how hard you've tried, you haven't measured up. And what's worse, *you never will.* Overexpecters don't say that, it oozes out of their frowns and glares. Sooner or later your motivation is sapped as demands and expectations replace excitement with guilt. The killer is that final moment when you realize you have become a weary slave of the impossible.

Fun fades. Laughter leaves. And what remains? This won't surprise anybody: The tyranny of the urgent. The uptight, the essential, the expected—*always* the expected. Which, being interrupted, means "the making of a coronary."

Because nobody screws up enough courage to tell overexpecters where to get off, these things keep happening:

The little child loses his love for art because he is told time and again to stop coloring outside the lines. Parents are often overexpecters.

The wife erodes in her joy around the house because she never seems to please the man she married. Husbands are often overexpecters.

The gifted and competent employee gets an ulcer because the boss finds it next to impossible to say two monosyllabic words, "good job." Employers are often overexpecters.

The once-dedicated, motivated pastor in a small church finally decides to change careers because he realizes he will never please them. Church members are often overexpecters.

The high school athlete chooses to hang it up at midseason because he knows that no matter what, he'll never satisfy. Coaches are often overexpecters.

And, yes, congregations get tired of being beaten and bruised with jabs, hooks, and uppercuts from pulpits. Preachers are often overexpecters.

Those of us who want to serve God need to buy out of this syndrome, by stopping the competition and beginning to enjoy life! Don't give in to overexpecters who want you to feel like an underachiever, and never make the standards of this world the measuring stick for your life, ministry, or achievements.

When you feel the pressure mounting as a taskmaster calls you to an ever-quickening pace, note that the antidote is simply peace of the kind only One can give. With these words He calls us to Himself: "Come to Me, all who are weary and heavy-laden, and I will give you rest" (Matthew 11:28). He doesn't speak of the world's burden, with all its unrealistic expectations, or those of a church, pastor, or board. Instead He offers a unique pace and standard: "Take My yoke upon you, and learn from Me, for I am gentle and humble in heart; and you shall find rest for your souls. For My yoke is easy, and My load is light" (vv. 29, 30).

Pride . . . prestige . . . personal needs . . . propriety . . . popular acclaim: None is good enough as a motive for Christian ministry. How colorless they seem against the background of Paul's challenge, "And whatever you do in word or deed, do all in the name of the Lord Jesus . . ." (Colossians 3:17).

As a young monk wrestling with some of the menial tasks assigned me within the monastery walls, I remember an older monk speaking of a young nun who worked at Father Damien's leper colony, on the island of Molokai. As she gave herself to the morning tasks of the infirmary, a reporter observed her dressing open wounds and oozing ulcers. With discomfort bordering on disgust, the man said, "Sister, I wouldn't do that for a million dollars." She looked at him, smiled sweetly, and softly said, "Neither would I!"

Let us have that kind of motive in our service to Christ, that every aspect of our individual and corporate lives might honor and glorify Him!

Finding the Right Motives

Surely the apostle Paul, who struggled with pride, prestige, personal needs, propriety, and personal acclaim, knew what it meant to have wrong motives for service. But he also outlines the fit motives that make us powerful witnesses for Christ.

Fear of God

In 2 Corinthians 5:11 Paul wrote, "Therefore knowing the fear of the Lord, we persuade men. . . ." Fearing God forms the first proper motive of service.

Evangelical and charismatic worship experiences have exhibited a refreshingly authentic informality and openness. But such an atmosphere also has one inherent danger: We know precious little reverence and awe for the Godhead.

God is awesome . . . like nothing and no one else. I am to fear Him, not with a servile fear—the horror a slave evidences in his master's presence. Rather I should show filial fear—the respect and love a son feels for his father. Because God *is* my Father, I am to reverence Him, considering His Person and purposes for my life . . . I am to be quiet and still in His presence.

Regularly we need reminders of God's singular awesomeness and the reverential fear due Him. "The fear of the Lord is the beginning of wisdom . . . ," but it is also the beginning of ministry (Proverbs 9:10). Paul's "Therefore knowing the fear of the Lord, we persuade men," shows us he would agree. The motive? fear of God. The ministry? persuading men.

When Paul uses the word *therefore*, he directs our attention to the verse before, in which he solemnly reminds us, "For we must all appear before the judgment seat of Christ, that each one may be recompensed for his deeds in the body, according to what he has done, whether good or bad."

We can expect to face two coming judgments. In the first, each of us will be asked to give account for what we have done with God's Son. Anyone who offers a faltering or negative answer will be separated from His Presence for eternity. The one who answers positively will have nothing held against him.

For believers, all judgment is past. We are not guilty and have an Advocate before the Father, who pleads in our behalf and affirms that there is no condemnation.

Beyond that, we face a final performance judgment. In his first letter to the Corinthian church, Paul wrote about being neither impressed nor intimidated by men's judging his motive or deeds: "But to me it is a very small thing that I should be examined by you, or by any human court; in fact, I do not even examine myself. I am conscious of nothing against myself, yet I am not by this acquitted; but the one who examines me is the Lord" (4:3, 4).

A chapter later Paul will write about the judgment, and he is fully aware that one day all our works will be revealed with fire, which will test all we've done. If the work is good, it will remain, and we will receive a reward. If the work is consumed by fire, we'll suffer loss.

In essence Paul says, though he is fully aware that men do and will judge, ultimately only the evaluation of God counts. With Him there are no secrets: He is *Lahai-roi,* "the God who sees everything." ". . . All things are open and laid bare to the eyes of Him with whom we have to do" (Hebrews 4:13). Regardless of the assessments of men, if we play our lives faithfully and with a sense of awe before our Lord, he assures us an imperishable crown lies in our future.

In light of Paul's words, I choose, amid all my struggles, to play my life before the Audience of One; and that decision gives me great freedom of ministry.

At one time it wasn't that way, though. When I served my first large church, I felt compelled to meet everyone's needs . . . and everyone seemed to need a part of me. My ministry became an eighteen-hour-a-day, seven-day week. It meant being away from my family at least six nights out of seven and coming in terribly late, to find my wife and kiddies in bed. A certain loneliness in the middle of a crowd began to overwhelm me. Much of what I did became a perfunctory performance; I went through the motions, because I allowed others to dictate my life.

They were tough years . . . and my family paid the price. Since then I've learned I cannot do it all . . . better yet, God never intended me to do it all. Father Hessberg, president of Notre Dame, was right when he said, "Cemeteries are filled with indispensable people." *Indispensable*— men and women the world couldn't get along without. But it has . . . and it will.

By the way, that large church I once pastored has done just fine without me. In many situations people are having their needs met by people other than the pastor—and they are learning!

As for me, I'm playing before that Audience of One. Fear of God—not of people—compels me to persuade others.

The Love of Christ

Second, Paul offers "for the love of Christ controls us . . ." as a proper motive for ministry (2 Corinthians 5:14). The context of that verse makes it clear we cannot do it on our own power, but His love—displayed on Calvary's cross—motivates, constrains, and controls us. Just as the fear of God compels us to persuade men, the love of Christ conditions us to love them.

As John writes:

> Beloved, let us love one another, for love is from God; and everyone who loves is born of God and knows God. The one who does not love does not know God, for God is love. By this the love of God was manifested in us, that God has sent His only begotten Son into the world so that we might live through Him. In this is love, not that we loved God, but that He loved us and sent His Son to be the

propitiation for our sins. Beloved, if God so loved us, we also ought to love one another.

1 John 4:7–11

We can only base our love on His. Because He loves us, a ministry of loving others can flow from us. Calvary love conditions us to love one another with divine love, which lies behind and beneath the ministry of caring and sharing that Christ intended to mark His church.

Re-creation in the Spirit

Third, Paul tells us, "Therefore if any man is in Christ, he is a new creature; the old things passed away; behold, new things have come" (2 Corinthians 5:17). He's talking about our own re-creation, which is uniquely the work of the Holy Spirit: "He saved us, not on the basis of deeds which we have done in righteousness, but according to His mercy, by the washing of regeneration and renewing by the Holy Spirit" (Titus 3:5).

The reality of our spiritual re-creation commends us to a watching world with a new ministry: reconciliation. "Now all these things are from God, who reconciled us to Himself through Christ, and gave us the ministry of reconciliation" (2 Corinthians 5:18). We are left among men to say, "The war is over . . . lay down your arms . . . see how He loves you and me."

Our pardon . . . peace . . . new purpose in life lead us to such a ministry. The change, the new creation, He's effected in our lives, now causes us to show the world how real Christ is. As we seek to minister, what we live out demonstrates that most authentically.

Our world longs to see the genuine article. The burns, the open wounds on the body of Jonah, caused by the gastric juices deep within that big fish, showed the authenticity of what God had done in his life and effected a ministry of reconciliation for an entire city.

As a reconciled and re-created people we have new

hearts within us. Those new hearts, broken as His is with pain for a wasting world, make us authentic as we tell people, "Be reconciled to God. . . ."

Applying Motives to Ministry

We may correlate our fit motives to God this way:

The fear of God	God the Father
The love of Christ	God the Son
Our re-creation by the Spirit	God the Spirit

One single motive for ministry, then—God!

Why do I serve Him? Because He is God . . . and God is love. Serving Him ought to express my love for Him. But only diligent self-scrutiny insures that I have pure motives, free from self. On a daily basis I need to ask myself:

Is My Ministry Selfless?

I need to take a look at my motives. Am I being *sincere?* That word comes from the Latin words *sine cera*, "without wax." When a Roman nobleman wanted to have a piece sculpted for his gardens, he would go down to the marketplace, meet with an artist, and tell him exactly what he wanted. For months, the sculptor gave himself to that task. Occasionally in the execution of his art, his hammer might fall just a little too heavily, or the chisel would slip, but for whatever reason just a little bit too much marble was taken off. Because they didn't have Elmer's Glue back then, the artist would take a clear wax, very much like our paraffin, heat it, apply it to the area affected, and shape it as he had orginally intended. The wax was clear, and the marble was so resilient, that it was almost impossible for the untrained eye to tell where the marble ended and where the wax began or if in fact there was any wax at all. So the first question the nobleman would ask when he came to view the masterpiece was: "Is it *sine cera?* Is it without wax?"

Have I done away with the wax in my life? Or do I have hidden, glossed-over motives?

A successful ministry must stem from a reverential awe for the Lord, in His Person and purpose for my life.

Is My Ministry Spontaneous?

Because I have experienced it in Christ, His love ought to pour out of me, flowing freely and faithfully on others. No one can force or regulate it; a new principle He has placed in me allows me to love and care for them.

At the end of Matthew's gospel, Jesus gives a surprising description of the judgment:

> But when the Son of Man comes in His glory, and all the angels with Him, then He will sit on His glorious throne. And all the nations will be gathered before Him; and He will separate them from one another, as the shepherd separates the sheep from the goats; and He will put the sheep on His right, and the goats on the left. Then the King will say to those on His right, "Come, you who are blessed of My Father, inherit the kingdom prepared for you from the foundation of the world. For I was hungry, and you gave Me something to eat; I was thirsty, and you gave Me drink; I was a stranger, and you invited Me in; naked and you clothed Me; I was sick, and you visited Me; I was in prison, and you came to Me."
>
> 25:31–36

The righteous, the sheep, give a reply that has always impressed me: ". . . Lord, when did we see You hungry, and feed You, or thirsty, and give You drink? And when did we see You a stranger, and invite You in, or naked, and clothe You? And when did we see You sick, or in prison, and come to You?" (vv. 37–39). How obvious they make it that their service was no premeditated bid for favors from God, but a spontaneous outpouring. The King's answer comes: ". . . Truly I say to you, to the extent that you did it to one of these brothers of Mine, even the least of them, you did it to Me" (v. 40).

Jesus carries on a similar dialogue with the goats, but He begins, ". . . Depart from Me, accursed ones, into the eternal fire . . . for I was hungry, and you gave Me nothing to eat; I was thirsty, and you gave Me nothing to drink, I was a stranger, and you did not invite Me in; naked, and you did not clothe Me; sick, and in prison, and you did not visit Me" (vv. 41–43).

When they ask, ". . . Lord, when did we see You hungry, or thirsty, or a stranger, or naked, or sick, or in prison, and not take care of You?" He answers, ". . . Truly I say to you, to the extent that you did not do it to one of the least of these, you did not do it to Me" (vv. 44, 45).

Both groups lived out the principle within them. The sheep have the principle of the Shepherd within, so they become as giving, caring, and loving as He is. The goats, who do not understand that principle, do not care, give, or love.

Only as far as we have experienced divine love can we demonstrate it to the world. Only when we have it as a part of our lives will our living and loving become spontaneous.

Is My Ministry Spirit Led?

Ministry must come not from obligation, but the liberation and leading of the Spirit. Because He re-creates us, God also energizes us for our share in the great ministry of reconciliation. As the Spirit speaks to us through the Word of God and cries out the needs of His people, we respond freely and faithfully.

As you seek to serve God, take time for a spiritual examination. Have you fallen into the traps of pride, prestige, personal needs, propriety, and popular acclaim? Or are you acting out of the right motives: fear of God, love of Christ, and re-creation in the Spirit? Is your ministry selfless, spontaneous, and Spirit led? These are the keys to lengthening your stride in ministry.

Four

Marriage—
Ideally and Really

Some people wonder whether I left my monastery to marry Rose. Though it would seem very romantic to say, "Yes, that's exactly the way it began," it wouldn't be accurate. Certainly the vow of chastity had bothered me enough to prompt me to leave, but I didn't meet Rose until almost two years later.

In 1965 after completing the Basic Agent Course at Fort Holabird, Maryland, I was assigned—quite by chance, I thought—to a crack intelligence agency in Washington, D.C. First I signed in at the 902nd INTC group; then I had to wait for all the initial clearances, because this unit coordinated very high level intelligence activities. Day after day, along with four other agents I had studied with, I endured an interminably long clearing process.

On one of those days, a young woman who looked like a secretary walked by. Something about her struck me—a beauty, simplicity, and purity I had seen in few women. As she passed the classified area, I remarked to a fellow agent, "I'm going to marry that girl!"

Though that may sound terribly vain and arrogant, I wasn't really so cocksure of myself. As a matter of fact, because of all my cloistered years, I felt rather awkward in social relationships. It took me six weeks to get up enough nerve to ask that woman out on a date!

On our first night, one question I asked was, "Are you Catholic?" I would not have dated anyone who was not. Yes, Rose answered, she had been a foster child, raised in an Italian Catholic home, where her delightful and devout foster mother took her to church. God's hand was in the plan, even then.

The special chemistry I felt on that date made me want to see her again. The following night I was scheduled to be in Pittsburgh, but I called to ask if I could see her when I returned . . . and she agreed. Seeing each other each evening became our pattern.

Early in our dating, we visited the Church of the Holy Family in Hillcrest Heights, Maryland. Night after night we approached a side altar, to light a votive candle and pray for personal purity and God's grace that we might not damage or disgrace our relationship.

Before long, we knew we would like to spend our lives together and began to think, dream, and plan toward that end. But before we could proceed I had to reach an equal footing with Rose. Soon after I met her I'd discovered Rose was not just a secretary. She was also in the army, assigned to the same intelligence group—and she outranked me! On June 30, when I was promoted, I caught up with her.

Two days later, as we knelt at that same side altar, I took her hand, slipped a ring on her finger, and asked if she would marry me.

We began to make plans for a December 26 church wedding, in which we could acknowledge the place faith had in our lives. In December my younger brother, a West Point cadet, could be my best man. Our plans continued in that direction until September 3. On my way home, that Friday evening, I stopped by Rose's. She and her roommates had taken an apartment in the same complex as I and my fellow agents. At the end of the day it was easy enough to walk over and meet to discuss our day's work.

That night she greeted me, "Guess who's on orders for Vietnam?"

Right then I knew I should never have volunteered! Twice I had submitted the army dream sheet and had requested assignment in the conflict zone. Now that my life had taken on special meaning, it had caught up with me, I thought. "Me?" I asked.

"No, not you," she responded, and I felt more at ease. But who was going?

"Don . . . Jim . . . Rod?" I named my roommates one by one. To each she answered, "No."

"I give up. Who's going?"

Almost in a whisper, she replied, "I am. . . ."

I couldn't believe they would even *think* of sending her to Vietnam. But one of our very good friends, the personnel officer in the unit, had confided that he had seen her name on a classified levy for assignment in Vietnam.

Not sure what to do, we called the personnel officer and asked if we could visit him that evening. He invited us to join him and his wife for dinner.

There was an out for Rose, he told us. Army regulations permitted a woman to ask for separation from service on the grounds of marriage. "Why not move up the wedding date?" Bob asked. Rose was scheduled to report no later than October 20, but if we hurried, we might get her name deleted from the orders.

I didn't have a lot of time. That night I called Dad and explained the dilemma. "Dad, I really don't know what to do. I need your advice."

"You do love her, don't you?"

"Absolutely!"

"Do you want to spend the rest of your life with her?"

"Most certainly!"

"Well, what are you waiting for?"

The next day we went to Father Noel Callahan at Holy Family Church and asked him to marry us the following Saturday, September 11. Once we explained the circumstances, he said they could waive the requirement of announcing the banns for three consecutive Sundays. He would meet with us each night that week for premarital counseling.

The next week was filled with high anticipation and excitement. The following Saturday, in the presence of God, with my mom and dad, my grandmother, and a few friends in attendance, the two of us became husband and wife.

For almost twenty-five years we have experienced many of the same rough seas others have encountered, but our little ship has weathered the storms—even a few big ones. Though we haven't always had smooth sailing, we've always had an exciting voyage.

Through the years we've learned a great deal: We are not squeaky clean and don't have it all together. We certainly are not experts, but God has enabled us to do some things right and has shown us where we've gone wrong.

Our real point of strength came into our marriage on March 30, 1968, when we committed our lives to Christ and asked Him to be Lord of the home we were struggling to build. Since then, many godly people have shared insight with us. What follows is simply a digest of what we have learned from a host of couples who have shared the beauty of their lives together.

Ideal or Real?

As I look back on those first weeks of marriage, I remember how many people thought we were the perfect couple. At one time or another, we have all heard, "Oh, they're such an ideal couple! They look as if they were made for each other. They just seem to fit together so nicely!" At times Rose and I really began to believe such statements. But since then, we've learned that quite a gap lies between the ideal and the real—and the Bible has a lot to say about both.

As Christians our marriages give us the opportunity to represent God, demonstrating to the world the kind of love He has for us. Let's not lose sight of the fact that marriage should mirror the love Christ has for the church as well as the love the church should have for God. In short, it becomes a picture of God's love affair with man.

God's initial instruction about marriage makes it quite clear a great difference exists between the ideal and the real:

> Then the Lord God said, "It is not good for the man to be alone; I will make him a helper suitable for him." . . . So the Lord God caused a deep sleep to fall upon the man, and he slept; then He took one of his ribs, and closed up the flesh at that place. And the Lord God fashioned into a woman the rib which He had taken from the man, and brought her to the man.
>
> Genesis 2:18, 21, 22

The Ideal

That first marriage involved no *uncertainty*. God specifically fashioned Eve for Adam, and neither could doubt the other was created for him or her.

Beyond that, there was no *incompatibility*. God took a rib from Adam and formed another who was completely other, yet from the beginning had been part of him. She was fashioned for him, formed from him, and neither needed to change. These brand-new humans didn't have a great deal of baggage to bring into that union—no scars of past guilt or memories of hurt.

Finally, there was no *iniquity*. The ideal marriage took place in the Garden of Eden. God fashioned each, pronounced them husband and wife—all in a sinless state. This description is in Genesis 2, and sin doesn't enter the picture until Genesis 3.

It was ideal. . . .

The Real

That ideal remains in the Garden, but those verses have principles we can apply to marriages today—to the *real*.

The Architect of marriage said, "For this cause a man shall leave his father and his mother, and shall cleave to his wife; and they shall become one flesh" (Genesis 2:24).

". . . A man shall leave his father and his mother . . ." implies *severance*. The young man or woman who wants to marry has to leave home, come out from under the rule of Mom and Dad, and begin a life linked to, but independent of them. By this very distinct act, a young person severs ties that bound him or her to Mom and Dad.

". . . And shall cleave to his wife . . . ," the verse continues. This speaks of *acceptance*. Two come together and embrace, just as they are—and being who they are is all right. Neither takes the other for the sake of potential— what either might become—but for what he or she is at that moment.

Each must have a commitment to allow the other to be an individual, not someone forced into a spouse's ideas of what ought to be. Each needs to take the other's ideas seriously and trust that he or she will be safe with this person. Though both change, they'll be free to become all God intended.

". . . And they shall become one flesh" describes *permanence*. From the start God saw marriage as an indissoluble bond. Over and over again Scripture teaches that marriage is most sacred. We are to take it seriously—and not just for a short period of time. Two becoming one take on a unity—a new identity. Breaking that means robbing something from each other . . . shattering each one's identity. The unity is to be kept intact.

Jump back to the start of the verse and note that it says, "For this cause. . . ." What cause? *Interdependence!* Verse 18 tells us God said, "It is not good for the man to be alone . . ." and verse 20 states, ". . . But for Adam there was not found a helper suitable for him." God fashioned a suitable companion, so the man would not be alone. He planned that they would be interdependent, that they would find completion in becoming one . . . and neither would be alone.

Making It Work

Any number of books will tell you how to build a better marriage . . . or how to terminate a troubled one. But most have missed out on two ideas from Solomon:

> By wisdom a house is built, And by understanding it is established; And by knowledge the rooms are filled With all precious and pleasant riches.
>
> Proverbs 24:3, 4

> For the Lord gives wisdom; From His mouth come knowledge and understanding.
>
> Proverbs 2:6

Did you catch that? Only by wisdom, understanding, and knowledge can a couple build a house, and those elements come only from God.

Considering practical precepts for building strong marriages requires that we closely study God's blueprint for them.

Blueprint for Women

The divine Architect of marriage speaks through the words of the apostle Paul to the Ephesian church:

> . . . Be subject to one another in the fear of Christ. Wives, be subject to your own husbands, as to the Lord. For the husband is the head of the wife, as Christ is the head of the church, He Himself being the Savior of the body. But as the church is subject to Christ, so also the wives ought to be to their husbands in everything.
>
> 5:21–24

In the context of submission to Christ and mutual submission, Paul gives a command to both wife and husband. The wife must submit to her husband and live for him. The husband should love his wife—and even die for her. Paul places Christ at the very center of that comparison. He is both the focus and the fulcrum. Keeping Christ as our focal point means we keep our eyes on Him. Having Him as the fulcrum means He provides balance in our marriage.

To the wife the command is stark—"be subject." But to help her understand, Paul compares it to the submission the church renders to Christ Himself.

Peter addresses the same issue in his first letter: "In the same way, you wives, be submissive . . ." (3:1). Many would like to change the word *submissive* or apologize for it, but there is no getting around it. It's a tough phrase.

Without spiritualizing too much, Christian women might do well to remember that submission exists in the Godhead. From it, we can get a clearer picture of how submission figures in the husband-wife relationship.

The Godhead has *ontological equality*. The Father is equal with the Son . . . the Son is equal with the Holy Spirit . . . the Holy Spirit is equal with the Father. Each is eternally coexistent and coequal with the other. Yet *functional subordination* exists. Jesus took upon Himself flesh, wrapping His divinity in humanity. He knew the pain and became sin for us, yet He remained equal with the Father. Despite the equality, in terms of his ministry, Jesus was functionally subordinate.

Scripture teaches that men and women in marriage have ontological equality. In Christ there is neither male nor female—total equality! But there is functional subordination. I don't know why, except that God says, "Wives, be submissive." And that is difficult.

Winning Behavior. What if a woman's husband is disobedient to God? Does that mean all bets are off? No. After telling wives to be submissive, Peter goes on to say, ". . . So that even if any of them are disobedient to the word, they may be won without a word by the behavior of their wives, as they observe your chaste and respectful behavior" (1 Peter 3:1, 2). Under the influence of such actions, husbands can't help but notice how their wives are living, and those unbelieving or disobedient men will be won back—*without a word!*

No preaching to them . . . no placing tracts under the ashtray . . . no rigging the car radio's buttons to the local Christian station . . . no arranging to have the pastor visit on the only weeknight the husband is home. None of this is necessary or desirable. As he observes chaste and respectful behavior, he will be won back.

In the next verse, Peter speaks of outward and inward beauty: "And let not your adornment be merely external—braiding the hair, and wearing gold jewelry, or putting on dresses." For too long many people have misunderstood this verse, and Christian women have almost shied away from any attempt to beautify themselves. Peter does not advocate that women totally forget their appearance, but that they not let all beauty be external.

By all means be attractive. It's part of being a godly woman, especially in a world where any man with 20/20 vision receives daily assaults, through the eye gate, from a series of seductive images that flash across his mind. The godly woman will do all she can to make herself attractive—pleasing and desirable to her husband.

To me, Rose is certainly lovely. I appreciate her modesty. She never dresses for other men and would never do anything that would detract from her Christian testimony. Yet she delights in making herself attractive for me. In the words of Proverbs 5, I am "exhilarated" . . . excited . . . turned on by her beauty.

Some women feel they are not beautiful, but the truly ugly person is that way on the inside. As a godly woman cares for every aspect of her appearance, without making it her major concern, the beauty God has built into her will shine forth.

Be submissive. Be attractive. Now, be supportive. In verse 4, Peter writes of the beauty in "the hidden person of the heart, with the imperishable quality of a gentle and quiet spirit, which is precious in the sight of God." This is the antithesis of the woman who tends to dominate her husband. How truly sad—and even uncomfortable to any perceptive observer—to see a woman who lords it over her husband. On the other hand, what a joy to see a woman willing to submit to his headship . . . supporting the leadership God has built into her husband . . . committed to bringing out the very best in her husband by allowing that inner beauty of a gentle and quiet spirit to shine forth.

Peter describes such demeanor as ". . . precious in the sight of God." This word *precious* is the same one he used to describe our redemption "with precious blood." God values the blood of Christ. When He looks at a godly woman and sees her supporting her husband, bringing out the best in him, through that gentle spirit, He says: "That's precious to Me."

Rose has taught me much from her gentle and quiet spirit. I wish I could tell you it has rubbed off on me, but I'm still learning from her.

One night I came home quite late, after making some pastoral calls. Rose had waited up, so I suggested we have a cup of my favorite winter drink: spiced tea. How delightful this drink feels on a cold evening, at the end of a long day. But Rose informed me we were out.

"No problem," I waved it aside. After all, how could she have known I wanted some? "But when you get a chance, pick up the ingredients, so we can have it on hand." I really thought I had handled the situation gracefully.

About a week or two later, we seemed to experience déjà vu. A cold winter night . . . I came home late . . . perfect time for a cup of spiced tea. When I suggested it, I knew from the look on Rose's face that something had registered. *She had not gotten the ingredients!*

That's when I made a scene that went something like this: "Rose, I don't believe it. I ask so little of you." At this point the frustrations of my entire day fused with my own martyr complex, and before long I began singing a litany of self-praise. "I never request special dinners. . . . I don't ask you to press my shirts in a special way. . . . I don't leave my socks all over the house. I asked you to do one thing . . . only one . . . and it wasn't important to you. Was it so much to ask?"

With that I stormed off to bed.

Now as a rule Rose and I try to honor Ephesians 4:26: ". . . Do not let the sun go down on your anger." We have drawn an imaginary line down the middle of our bed and have an agreement to meet there each night, as a reminder that there are to be no divisions between us.

That was easy to do in a double bed, but with the advent of king-sized ones, we had to make a conscious effort to meet. Well, that night I didn't want to be anywhere near the middle. As a matter of fact, I moved to the very edge on my side. Had Rose touched me with a feather, I probably would have fallen off. She was right in the middle; then she came over to me; but I wouldn't budge—I don't know why. Stubbornly, I felt a need to express my disappointment.

The next morning I still smarted from the evening before. Not ready to get out of the sulks, I didn't kiss her as I usually do. I just got up and started my normal routine, which is quite regimented. Rose had studied me well.

First I brush my teeth. As I went to grab my toothbrush, I found this note taped to the toothpaste: "John, I appreciate the loving touches you give our marriage. Touch here, touch there. You are the cinnamon, Tang, lemonade, tea, clove, sugar of my life."

She's pretty cute, I thought. *But why didn't she get that cinnamon, Tang, lemonade, tea, clove, and sugar, to make that spiced tea, the way I asked her?*

Next I reached for the shaving cream, only to find another note: "John I love and appreciate the quality of husband, father and minister you are. You guessed it. You're the spice of my life!"

When I stepped into the shower, I half expected another note, but there was none. When I finished, I went to the dresser, and leaning against a picture, I found number three: "John, I appreciate all the time you give to me, doing the things that are important to me. You *really are* the spice of my life!"

In the top drawer, on my socks, I found a simpler note: "You're the spice of my life. Rose."

With my shorts I found another reminder: "I appreciate

the thoughtful ways you show me that you love me. John, you're the spice of my life. (Over.)" As I turned to the other side, I read: "I'll wash your other shorts. Rose."

I went to our walk-in closet and pulled the light switch. The paper I found in my hand said: "John, I appreciate your taking out the garbage. You are the spice of my life. Rose."

Persistent woman!

I put on my slacks, shirt, and reached for my tie . . . "John, I appreciate you. You're the spice of my life and of our girls' as well."

I looked over at her, still and peaceful in bed. To this day I wonder if she really was sleeping or just enjoying it all more than I know. Still, I wasn't ready to give in.

Being very spiritual minded, I went downstairs for my devotions. As I opened my Bible to our reading in Proverbs, one last note appeared: "John, I love all your habits. Your dogs, your trips, etc., etc., etc. You are the spice of my life!"

Guilty! Even in the first note, I'd realized I'd made a to-do about nothing. Yet in her own godly way, she broke me down. I went upstairs, kissed her, held her in my arms, and told her how special she was. Rose has a way of supporting me, even when I've acted very, very small.

In his final admonition, Peter says the godly woman will be attentive. "Thus Sarah obeyed Abraham, calling him lord, and you have become her children if you do what is right without being frightened by any fear" (1 Peter 3:6). She obeyed, being attentive to his desires and needs.

I've heard that the greatest American male need is affirmation and appreciation from his own wife. Many times she loses sight of the fact that she alone has been appointed by God to meet her husband's very special needs.

Too often a woman becomes overbusy, torn in many directions because she is wife, mother, a significant person in church—and possibly a full-time-job holder. In a hectic world, she must carefully hoard some energies, so that she does not fail to care for her husband. How much I appreciate the attention Rose gives me and my ministry.

At times a sense that everything important to me also is important to her overwhelms me. Without her, I simply couldn't function very well.

In six verses God tells the godly woman: You've got to be submissive . . . attractive . . . supportive . . . and attentive. Now what does He say to men?

Blueprint for Men

Paul has a command for men as well:

> Husbands, love your wives, just as Christ also loved the church and gave Himself up for her; that He might sanctify her, having cleansed her by the washing of water with the word, that He might present to Himself the church in all her glory, having no spot or wrinkle or any such thing; but that she should be holy and blameless. So husbands ought also to love their own wives as their own bodies. He who loves his own wife loves himself.

> Ephesians 5:25–28

Husbands are to love their wives as Christ loved the church. Jesus died for the church, spending all His energies for her, so He might one day sanctify and present her to God, unblemished because of His care for her.

Any Christian man who seeks to live that way in his marriage will also find it a tough commandment. It's not a matter, as some might suspect, of God making marriage harder for women!

Peter, too, has something to say to men. Into just one verse he packs many powerful ideas: "You husbands likewise, live with your wives in an understanding way, as with a weaker vessel, since she is a woman; and grant her honor as a fellow-heir of the grace of life, so that your prayers may not be hindered" (1 Peter 3:7).

". . . Live with your wives," he commands us. In other words, husband, be aware your wife is there. How often have you taken her for granted?

At the end of a hectic day, does a man come home and lose sight of the fact that the woman who loves him and is deeply committed to him has probably had an equally busy day? He's home, his work has ended, at least for a time . . . but hers continues. Frequently he's had strokes in the marketplace, but has she received any? As the two meet at the end of the day, they should experience a sharing of lives that says to her, "I am truly aligned with you. We are one." To a woman, this kind of sensitivity is essential.

Though "live with your wives" seems a fairly obvious statement, it has a much deeper meaning. Peter really means share life with them—fully and freely.

Not only do we need awareness of our wives, we must understand them: ". . . live with your wives in an understanding way. . . ." Understanding comes as a by-product of sharing our lives with our wives. As we live in depth, we gain an ever-deepening knowledge of how they think and feel. But to do that, we have to listen and become sensitive. And that won't just happen. . . .

Over the years I have studied to learn Rose. I know her on the phone. I can tell a great deal about how she feels by looking into her eyes . . . sitting across the table from her . . . holding her hand. I have committed myself to learning what it takes to fulfill her life. Her cares, her needs, where her heart really is, the involvement she has with her Lord, the way she has her total being wrapped up with our children . . . I know something of all these. Yet because Rose is on the cutting edge—the growing edge—of life, I haven't learned her fully. The process continues, and I delight in coming to understand the woman I love.

Knowing who she is, though, is not quite enough. Learning about her day-in and day-out schedule also helps. Recently Rose went away for a week, with our oldest daughter, Laurie. While she was gone, I had the privilege of filling in for her—playing both father and mother. Though I always felt I had an appreciation for how much Rose does, that week taught me a lot. . . .

Monday was ballet. Tuesday, before I took the younger ones to school, I had to dash to the dry cleaners, the

Laundromat, and the shoe repairman. After driving Natalie and Jana to their schools, I got back just in time to teach Rose's Bible-study class to more than a hundred women. Tuesday afternoon meant piano lessons. Wednesday was chorus for one, band for the other. Thank God for fast foods! Thank God for two little girls who understand Daddy could never really fill in for Mommy.

Spending a day or two becoming familiar with our wives' schedules might be a great exercise. We'll learn a great deal about them . . . and will probably become much more understanding.

How do we live with our wives? ". . . As with a weaker vessel. . . ." Many women might like an exact explanation of that phrase. I wish I could provide one! Now, I see it as a charge from Peter for us men to be strong. As head of the home, the man has been charged by God to protect his wife. Though that has a material side, it is also spiritual. A man's spiritual strength can erect a shield around his house that protects those he loves from influences that could erode commitment to Christ and to the common goals of that marriage and family. The husband who takes seriously the matter of spiritual leadership and spends time developing Christlike qualities, through prayer, Bible study, and family worship, intensifies that protection.

Several years ago, at a weekend retreat for singles, I asked a large group what women wanted most in their mates. After several people had made suggestions, one young woman, who obviously had it together in many parts of her life, said, "What I look for most in the man with whom I'd like to spend the rest of my life before God is one who will lead me in my walk with God."

She had a proper spiritual perspective!

As a Christian husband how should you treat your wife? Peter challenges you to ". . . grant her honor as a fellow heir of the grace of life, so that your prayers may not be hindered."

That's not all the Bible has to say about wives. Solomon said: "He who finds a wife finds a good thing, And obtains favor from the Lord" (Proverbs 18:22). Ecclesiastes

9:9 promises, "Enjoy life with the woman whom you love all the days of your fleeting life which He has given to you under the sun; for this is your reward in life, in your toil in which you have labored under the sun." Clearly God gives a man a wife to show His favor and tells him to enjoy life with her—to love her . . . and demonstrate that love.

Sometimes we are so slow to show love to our wives. We may take them for granted. They have been here yesterday . . . and the day before . . . and today. When was the last time we tried to show them how precious they are?

In recent months I delighted in watching the romance of our oldest daughter, who married a young minister. I saw their tremendous affection and great respect for each other. As they relived all those areas of my early courtship with Rose, they reminded me how I've begun to take her for granted.

Several months ago, as I waited to meet one of my daughters at a New York airport, I couldn't help but notice one man. Under normal circumstances, I would have over-looked this simply dressed man, who was short, in his mid-fifties, with gray hair, and dark, horn-rimmed glasses that concealed a hearing aid. In a crowd of hundreds of people, I never would have seen him, if I hadn't picked up on the fact that he was waiting for Ethel. I saw it in his eyes—a look of loving anticipation—*and* it was written all over the balloons he carried. Right smack in the middle of TWA's grand concourse, he sported three helium filled spheres: *Welcome home, Ethel . . . I missed you, E.T. . . . I love Ethel!*

Good for him! This man loved his wife . . . wanted to show her . . . and didn't care if the whole world witnessed his demonstration; somehow he wanted Ethel to know it was okay if everyone knew how special she was to him.

A Costly Challenge

Finally, we must make building a strong marriage a high priority in our lives. As we each consider personal priorities, we must ask: *What preferential rating should I give to the persons and things to which I must be committed?*

Certainly our greatest commitment must be to Jesus Christ—knowing . . . loving . . . and serving Him. Second only to that is marriage—I believe God would have us order our priorities this way. Through marriage God can make a statement to the world of His love for all people. He's made it clear that the union of husband and wife ought to mirror the love Jesus has for His Bride, the church. How awesome, to think that when we invest in our marriages that way, we represent God to a watching world.

As we do that we need to keep some things in mind. . . .

Unabated Efforts

First, it takes unabated and unaborted efforts to strengthen a marriage. Even in the face of immense difficulties, don't slacken your attempts to build a great marriage. Don't quit—it's always too soon! God says, "Hang on, My child."

Maybe you think you've tried everything, but until you try it His way, you have not exhausted all the possibilities. I would not for one minute minimize the pain some people feel in their marriages, but neither can I underestimate His grace. Had Rose and I not come to Christ and so renewed our commitment to each other, I doubt our marriage would have survived the early storms. As rich and enjoyable as I find my life with Rose, despite all its struggles, I remain convinced both husband and wife need to make unceasing efforts to keep a marriage in good condition.

Unbroken Promises

Achieving any goal takes dedication, and building a marriage is one of the greatest of human endeavors. Apart from the commitment to the promises we articulate to our mates, we cannot construct a God-honoring union. Unbroken promises gladden God's heart. Unless we daily recommit ourselves to our spouses, keeping to our vows, we will not have lasting, happy, blessed marriages.

Unconditional Love

Unconditional love brightens each day and lightens the way. Working with young couples preparing for marriage excites me: They never seem to notice each other's faults.

But I find it even more exciting to sit with those who have loved for years . . . know each other full well . . . bear some battle scars . . . yet have an intact love—stronger, deeper, purer than ever. Such unconditional love makes up godly marriages.

In the two years before Dad's death, he battled several medical problems, including a cancer that surfaced in at least two places. This, along with asthma, required different medications—some of them mood altering. Even though Mom's an up person and Dad was quiet and gentle, they had some trying days. Rather than sending him a card, on Dad'seventieth birthday Mom wrote a love letter:

> *Ed,*
> *I love you when you are tolerant. . . .*
> *I love you when you are kind. . . .*
> *I love you when you look serene. . . .*
> *I love you when you are happy.*
> *I love you when you have a happy face. . . .*
> *I love you when you clown. . . .*
> *I love you when you talk seriously. . . .*
> *I love you the way you look dressed up. . . .*
> *I love you when you are soft. . . .*
> *I love you when you are considerate. . . .*
> *I love you when you are caring. . . .*
> *I love you when you are gentle. . . .*
> *And, my darling,*
> *When you are none of the things above,*
> *I become hurt,*
> *frustrated,*
> *concerned,*
> *and crushed*
> *all because I overlove you.*
> *I truly love you.*
> *Anne*

Undeniable Dedication

As Mom and Dad prepared to celebrate their fiftieth wedding anniversary, I think they would have told their children, grandchildren, and great-grandchild that it takes unabated and unaborted effort . . . unbroken promises . . . and unconditional love, but they'd also have agreed that it takes something more. . . .

Christian marriage also requires undeniable dedication to the lordship of Jesus Christ, which deepens a spouse's ties to Him and consequently to his or her mate. Jesus becomes the focal point, the very center of the love relationship.

Even as I pen these words, I desire all that in the life and love I share with Rose. Then I pray it will become a blessed reality in the lives of Laurie and her husband, Lance. When God brings my daughters Natalie and Jana to that point, I pray it for them, too.

Finally, I pray it for you, who have taken time to ponder these pages.

Five

Learning to Be a "We"

My Dear Family—

I just want to let you all know that you are more special to me than you could imagine. . . .

I've been thinking about you lately. I guess that's mainly because I see myself doing things that are a part of growing up. And that scares me, because in some cases, that means growing apart from your family. Well, not in this case. I'm praying that God will allow us to grow closer through the years.

It makes me want to cry to write like this, because it makes me feel like an "I" writing from the outside to a "you" in the inside, who are really a "we" without "me." So let's be one big "we"! Okay?

I'm learning more and more every day that when all is said and done, it's really your family that matters, and I want to treat you that way always.

Looking forward to spending this weekend being a "we."

I love you all. . . .

Laurie

(a small part of a great "we")

At the beginning of her sophomore year of college, my daughter Laurie wrote us that treasure of a letter that reflected just what it meant to her to be part of our family. Her feelings reflect the needs of all people to be part of a great, loving "we"—the family.

Finding the Right Focus

For years I preached on the importance of building a strong family and its significant role in the church. But I was just preaching it. . . .

More recently I made my greatest earthly commitment, not to the building of the church of Jesus Christ, but the building of my family. Looking back over fifteen years of ministry, I realized that when my life is over, few people in the little church in Windsor, Vermont, will remember me . . . the army chaplaincy will never mourn my passing . . . the Trinity College administration will not write my obituary . . . the people at that larger church in New Jersey may even forget how to spell my name.

But when they put me in a box and prepare to lower me into the ground, three young ladies will be ready to pen a summary of my life. The feelings and memories that flood their minds will determine whether or not I've been successful as a dad. So I'm committed to playing my earthly life to that audience of three:

Laurie, our firstborn, who has been blessed with so many special gifts and talents. Natalie Anne, our middle child who has her mother's softness and gentleness, with a deep, abiding sensitivity toward others. She and I share an interest in animals and the hobby of breeding, raising, and showing Golden Retrievers. Over the years, we've become very good friends. When a teacher assigned her to write a poem to a special friend, Natalie penned this:

This is a poem to John, my dad
Who has shared with me most of the experiences I've had.

> *Although I don't understand the discipline I've received,*
> *To know you loved me anyway made me feel relieved.*
> *Oh, and then our hobby—even though we seldom won,*
> *It rarely mattered as long as we had fun.*
> *Remember going store to store,*
> *Only to see what we had seen before?*
> *And the way you're teaching me how to live,*
> *Is something that one day I hope to give.*
> *You not only instructed me from day to day,*
> *You shared your life with me in a most special way.*

Jana Marie, our third and youngest, who seems the divine exclamation point in our family. She has a desire to give so much to her family. Not uncommonly, she goes into her room, takes something very precious to her, wraps it up, and gives it to another member of the family.

Rose and I truly thank God for the three precious daughters He entrusted to us. We also delight in the many things we have learned—and are learning—about the priorities and privileges of parenting.

Not for one minute do my wife and I think we have attained perfection as parents, but we have made a commitment to try to be what God wants us to be for one another. If you polled our children, I am confident each girl would say that we try. As Laurie once told me, in a note, "Daddy, you *are* trying . . . very trying."

Several years ago, I heard one of the Gaithers recite a poem that truly embodied the deepest feelings of my heart in regard to my children. I jotted it down as best I could, adapted it to fit my own family situation, and to this day carry it with me wherever I go. I've read it to audiences across the country and have literally given out hundreds of copies of it. I'd like to share it with you:

> *I may never be as clever as my neighbor down the street.*
> *I may never own the riches of some other men I meet.*
> *I may never earn the glory that other men have had. . . .*
> *But you know I've just got to be successful as my little girls' dad!*

There are certain dreams I cherish, that I'd like to see come true.
And there are things I'd accomplish, ere my working time is
*   through.*
But the task my heart is set on is to guide through good and bad . . .
And make me successful as my little girls' dad.

Oh, I may never come to glory and may never gather gold.
And men may count me a failure when my earthly life is told.
But if these little ones who follow after shall be godly, kind,
*   and true, then I'll be glad . . .*
Because I'll know I've been successful as my little girls' dad.

Tis the one job I dream of, the task I think of most.
For if I fail these girls, I've nothing else to boast.
For the wealth and fame I'd gather, my future would be sad . . .
If I fail to be successful as my little girls' dad.

An Obligation

I see ordering of our priorities to include an important place for the family as a mandate from God Himself. As my favorite verse says, "Train up a child in the way he should go, Even when he is old he will not depart from it" (Proverbs 22:6).

For too long Christian parents have numbly believed this verse unconditionally guarantees that if they register their child into the church cradle roll as soon as he arrives . . . see to it he slips into his spot in the nursery on Sunday morning . . . make up part of the audience when he sings "Christmas Bells" with the beginner department . . . sacrifice to send him to a Christian school . . . send him to a Christian camp each summer . . . open their home to the Youth Fellowship . . . they need not feel overly concerned about his eternal destiny. Even if he has a prolonged period of rebellion in his life, they believe this verse promises they will eventually see him come back to the truth.

While all these elements can be good for a child's spiritual formation, there is so much more to it. . . .

Understanding the Mandate

This promise falls nicely into four parts:

> Train up. . . .
> . . . A child. . . .
> . . . In the way he should go. . . .
> . . . When he is old he will not depart
> from it.

Train up.   The Hebrew word picture suggested by "train up" is that of placing a bit in a horse's mouth, for the purpose of bringing it into submission.

In its noun form, the word depicts a midwife's role. Just prior to the delivery, she prepared a sweet paste by crushing and blending dates and other fruits. After cleaning the newborn, but before presenting the child to the mother, she dipped a finger into the paste and rubbed it gently over the baby's lips and gums, the inside of the mouth, and the soft palate. This stimulated the sucking instinct and created a thirst within the child.

Proverbs 22:6 really says, then, that Christian parents ought to nurture their child's inborn longing for God. Each person has that desire for Him, and it falls to each parent to encourage that thirst for Him.

A child.   In English, this term encourages us to take the idea behind it lightly. We think of a *child* as a little one, who must be taken by the hand to cross the street. The Greek word *paidion* pictures just that, too. But the Hebrew word is *na'ar*. The Old Testament uses it to describe Ichabod at his birth (1 Samuel 4:21) . . . Samuel at three or four, when he was being weaned from his mother (1 Samuel 1:24) . . . the preteen Ishmael (Genesis 21:16) . . . Joseph at seventeen (Genesis 37:2) . . . Shechem, at the age of his marriage (Genesis 34:19) . . . and Absalom the warrior (2 Samuel 18:5). In reality this word takes us from infancy to adulthood!

What does this show us? that the parent is intended by God to foster that thirst for spiritual things from infancy through adulthood. No parent can abdicate that role, even when the child leaves his or her roof.

Grandparents also need to see the privilege and responsibility they have to nurture a commitment to spiritual things in the lives of their grandchildren. Apart from Rose and myself, the single greatest force in our children's lives has been the involvement of my mom and dad in their growth. Because my parents have a real love for both God and our daughters, the girls often go to their grandparents for counsel and comfort.

As I watch our young grandsons, Allen and Andrew, my parents' model challenges me. From the start, I want to be involved in their lives. Instead of becoming the crotchety old man who sits back in a chair, reading a newspaper or watching television and barking out monosyllabic answers to their questions, I want to hold them close, lock eyes with them and listen to them now, so that later I can do those same things and have them want to listen to me. In short, I want to be their friend, so that one day I can tell them about my Friend, Jesus.

In the way he should go.   This next phrase speaks not just of *a* way, but *the* way.

God has a unique and personal plan for each person. Every child is unique—there are no carbon copies. Too often we think of children in terms of other people: daddy's little girl, or a boy who has mommy's eyes. Actually each child has individual peculiarities and talents, endowed by God.

The godly parent carefully studies each child, to understand his or her God-given gifts, then helps that child become all God intends.

The word translated "way" in this verse also appears in Proverbs 30:18: "There are three things which are too wonderful for me, Four which I do not understand: The way of an eagle in the sky, The way of a serpent on a rock, The way of a ship in the middle of the sea, And the way of a man with a maid." Each of these ways is very different. An eagle soaring through the sky cannot compare to a ship cutting through the sea. A snake darting across a rock has little, in common with a young man's way with a maiden (it better have little in common, if she happens to be one of my daughters!).

Just as each has an individual character, so every child has his or her own way, too. Parents need to foster it right through adulthood, helping each child to find *the* path God has outlined.

Even when he is old he will not depart from it.   Here the Hebrew gives us another word picture. "When he is old" speaks of the time when a young man has hair on his face, is seen as an adult, ready to go out on his own. At this critical point in a child's development, God's Word assures that if parents have fostered an interest in spiritual things, when the child goes off on his own, they will see him continue in the path God has outlined for him.

Not too long ago, I went through a little box in which I keep some of my earthly treasures. Among them is a "Four Spiritual Laws" booklet that has special significance for me.

I regularly taught the eighth-grade pastor's instruction class, and I used this booklet in the final lesson, because it gives a clear presentation of the gospel and an opportunity for each student to personally embrace the Lord Jesus.

Every place where the booklet has the word *you*, I encouraged students to fill in their own names.

When Laurie went off to college, she gave me her booklet with the name filled in. Beneath the prayer, accepting Christ as Savior, she wrote, "Age three, when I was so ill. Again at age six, when I understood it more. Now each day I recommit my life."

I thank God for Laurie and her obvious sincerity in her commitment to Him. Often I have told her how grateful Rose and I are for the purity of life and godly example she set for her sisters. Never has she done anything that made it difficult for me to step into the pulpit.

But even though our children are older, our task is not done . . . our influence is not over. The verse from Proverbs reminds Rose and me that God requires constant and consistent investment of our lives in Laura, Natalie, and Jana.

Giving Our Children a Message

Once a great missionary wrote his children:

> I have had many a sorrow of heart and it still remains
> one of my chief regrets that I have not been able to give
> myself to mother and you children more. The harvest is
> great and the laborers few which means there have been
> many calls upon me. I do not justify my negligence, but
> any sacrifice made by you for our dear Lord Jesus' sake has
> not be unrewarded.

Though many have lifted up this man's zeal, telling missionaries and ministers he showed the greatest form of commitment, I belive we must reexamine such seemingly admirable sentiments and find them much at fault.

Too often I have seen the pathways of homes strewn with the wreckage of young lives, because Daddy or Mommy became too busy as a minister or Christian worker. They handed little John and Mary a message all right: *You aren't important—to me or God!* Though the parents probably didn't mean it to read that way, they gave the impression nonetheless, and the family suffered. Sadly, often the details they placed before family could have been handled by another person.

Never can the work of the church come before building strong, godly families, because without them, we can only build a weak, fragmented church that reflects the state of our intimate circles of living.

"You aren't important" is not the message God had in mind to present through the family. Communicating His love and caring to our children ought to become a primary objective. You can't do that by long distance or empty decree. It takes declarative example.

God's plan for parenting by modeling appears in Deuteronomy 6:5–7:

> And you shall love the Lord your God with all your heart
> and with all your soul and with all your might. And these

> words which I am commanding you today, shall be on
> your heart; and you shall teach them diligently to your
> sons and shall talk of them when you sit in your house and
> when you walk by the way and when you lie down and
> when you rise up.

Even that doesn't mean we simply limit our modeling to
sitting in the house, taking a walk, putting children to
bed, and waking them in the morning. As the words of
the Great Shemah become imprinted upon our hearts, we
live our love for God from the inside out—we become
full-time models of living faith.

Chuck Swindoll told me the story of a young missionary
mother who was in Japan during the Second World War.
As soldiers went through the city, looking for Americans
or any other hostile peoples, they came upon the abandoned building where this woman hid.

In her arms she held her infant daughter. Her little boy,
terrified by the sounds of war thundering around him,
stood close by, clinging tightly to his mother's skirts. Suddenly soldiers came to the door and began pounding on it
with their rifle butts. If they were able to break it down,
the missionary realized, she and her children might become one of the atrocities of war.

Holding her baby tightly, she pulled the little boy closer.
Despite the horrifying sounds outside, she began to sing
ever so softly:

> *He leadeth me! O blessed thought!*
> *O words with heav'nly comfort fraught!*
> *Whate'er I do, where'er I be,*
> *Still 'tis God's hand that leadeth me.*

Finally morning came, the noise died down, and the soldiers were gone. The little boy walked over to the door
and just touched it. As he did, the heavy steel door that
had shielded them fell outward off its hinges!

The little boy—now a great Christian leader and
statesman—never forgot the sounds of war or the song of

the woman. The faith his mother modeled when she sang those sweet words of confidence marked him for life.

Being a Model

What specific steps can we take when we model faith for our children? I'd like to talk about seven lessons we can show them through our own lives.

Lesson 1: Teach the Love of God

By loving God ourselves, we can show our children what it means to live out that love. When God first gives them to us, children are so pliable and eager to follow our example. Though we say "Love God," if we don't model it in our lives, they will never learn it.

As a military chaplain, I found that young men and women felt most comfortable with me when they could set aside the military. So occasionally I wore a clerical shirt rather than my uniform.

One Sunday, after returning to my quarters, I took off that shirt and collar and changed into casual clothes. When Rose called the family for dinner, four-year-old Natalie entered wearing my clerical shirt, with the white collar in place. Though it went from her shoulders to the floor, that didn't matter. Somehow her identification with Daddy and what he represented was more important.

Kids observe us—and they miss very little. They easily discern if we are authentic—if love for God invades every facet of our daily living. Children who see God as close, loving, available, and kind more easily begin a love relationship with Him. It's best modeled up close!

Lesson 2: Teach the Word

Too many parents have abdicated their role as teachers of the Word of God, allowing the Sunday-school teacher, youth pastor, and senior pastor to rule in their children's spiritual lives.

Whether or not we like it, our attitude toward the day-to-day relevance of His Word becomes apparent to our children. If we seem too busy to make time for it in our lives, they will not hide the Word of God in their hearts, and it will not help them in trials and temptations.

Often, we are not the students of God's Word we should be, but what the writer of Hebrews describes:

> For though by this time you ought to be teachers, you have need again for someone to teach you the elementary principles of the oracles of God, and you have come to need milk and not solid food. For everyone who partakes only of milk is not accustomed to the word of righteousness, for he is a babe.

> Hebrews 5:12, 13

Too many Christians expect to be fed the way a mother bird feeds her young; they live on regurgitated truth, instead of getting into the Word, doing their own study, chewing it up, digesting it themselves. Only when they have fresh insight into the Word can parents pass on both the process and reality of God to their children. So make Bible study a regular part of your life.

The Book of Ecclesiastes concludes: ". . . Fear God and keep His commandments, because this applies to every person" (Ecclesiastes 12:13). To keep His commandments, you have to *know* them. For children to know them, they must be taught—by parents!

Lesson 3: Teach Obedience

Knowing and teaching are only starting points, however. Action has to follow them. Jesus said, "If you know these things, you are blessed if you do them" (John 13:17). Blessedness—happiness—comes as a consequence of fulfilling the Word of God. As we realize the fullness of life it brings, we ought to feel prompted to be obedient ourselves and to teach our children the delights of obedience.

Parents who want their children to walk in the light of God's law might share this prayer of the Psalmist: "Teach me to do Thy will, For Thou art my God; Let Thy good Spirit lead me on level ground" (143:10). When we model submission to God's Word and will, we teach our children the principle of accountability. As a child is not fully prepared for this life without a knowledge of the laws of his nation, so no one can face life in eternity without accountability to the laws of the Lord.

Lesson 4: Teach Balance

Because our world staggers and reels in its own imbalance, we need to teach our children to have a balance based on God. In one very tender narrative, Luke describes Jesus' relationship to his parents and the balance that became apparent in His life: "And He went down with them, and came to Nazareth; and He continued in subjection to them; and His mother treasured all these things in her heart. And Jesus kept increasing in wisdom and stature, and in favor with God and men" (Luke 2:51, 52).

One of my daughters attends a public school that has a program in which selected youngsters, the accelerated students, shadow corporate executives. The purpose is to give the teens some idea of what it's like to be in the business sector.

But doesn't that come soon enough in life? Can't we allow them to be children while they are still young? We owe it to them to protect their childhood from society's pressure-cooker pace. Do we need to wonder that so many children require therapy, when they deal with pressures they can't handle and finally consider suicide as an option?

We need to give our children this balance of mind, body, spirit, and social and emotional well-being. Without shoving them into adulthood before their time, we need to provide a broad background of experience that makes balanced growth possible.

Lesson 5: Teach Humility

As we teach children of God's love, we must not lose perspective on the role humility plays in our modeling. At times we Christians have set ourselves both *apart* from the world and *above* it. When Paul discerned such haughtiness in the Corinthian church, he wrote them sharply:

> Do you not know that the unrighteous shall not inherit the kingdom of God? Do not be deceived; neither fornicators, nor idolators, nor adulterers, nor effeminate, nor homosexuals, nor thieves, nor the covetous, nor drunkards, nor revilers, nor swindlers shall inherit the kingdom of God. And such were some of you; but you were washed, but you were sanctified, but you were justified. . . .

> 1 Corinthians 6:9–11

We cannot take our names off that list—only Christ, who washed, sanctified, and justified us can do that. Once we realize where we came from, we can accept others just as they are—the way He accepted us!

No one is an accident of birth; each human was formed by the Maker God, of whom David said: "For Thou didst form my inward parts; Thou didst weave me in my mother's womb. I will give thanks to Thee, for I am fearfully and wonderfully made; Wonderful are Thy works, And my soul knows it very well" (Psalms 139:13, 14).

Ultimately each one of us comes from the divine hand, and we are what we are by God's grace. As we parents reflect that attitude in our lives, our children can pick up on it.

Lesson 6: Teach Sensitivity

After reminding the scribe that first and foremost he should love God, Jesus told him to love his neighbor as himself. In order to do that, he had to develop sensitivity to those around him. Likewise, before we can teach children how to be sensitive, we have to learn that lesson ourselves. Can we show by our own actions that we have the needs of others on our hearts and minds?

During the days of the great railroads, a young boy

traveled with his daddy on the Phoenix Chief. As their train made its way across the country, a black porter served their compartment. One day the boy noticed the man coming out of his daddy's compartment with tears in his eyes.

Bothered by that, the boy asked, "Did my daddy hurt you?"

The big black man stooped, locked eyes with the boy, and answered, "No, your daddy didn't hurt me. He saw me limping and asked what the problem was. When I told him, he invited me into your compartment, had me sit down, and took off my sock and shoe. After examining the infection, he lanced it, cleaned it, and put a dressing on. As he began putting on my sock and shoe, your daddy asked me if I loved Jesus. I told him I didn't, but that Mommy had. Right then I realized that if this white man could love me that way, then Jesus must have really loved me the way my mommy had said."

No wonder that little boy grew up committed to caring, his spirit sensitized to the pain of others. One day he became president of the Billy Graham Evangelistic Association, because he caught the sensitivity his daddy's faith taught.

Lesson 7: Teach Self-control

Finally, in an out-of-control world, we need to teach our children self-control. Though we find it listed in the fruit of the Spirit, "But the fruit of the Spirit is love, joy, peace, patience, kindness, goodness, faithfulness, gentleness, self-control . . ." (Galatians 5:22, 23), we often lack the moderation required of us. As with other things, our children quickly pick up on our lack of restraint and are more likely to do what they see than what they hear.

If they don't hear of self-control from us, where will such teaching come from? Rarely does an age that seems to thrive on lack of discipline talk of it. Even within the church how often do we hear of the beauty of self-control? Yet it is one of the hallmarks of the spiritual person. In fact, until we commit ourselves to becoming disciplined throughout our lives, we will not have it in our spiritual lives!

Somehow I link my weight struggle to my earlier monastic days, when we rose at two each morning to chant the first hours of the divine office. Years later, I still find myself waking at that hour.

Then I do battle with myself for what seems a very long time, before I give up and go downstairs for something to eat. I'm such a volitional cripple that I've even lied about it. Often Rose wakes and asks where I'm going, and I tell her I'm heading for a drink of water. I might even mean that when I say it, but by the time I get downstairs, I devour anything I can lay my hands on. As a result, I've gone up and down on the weight elevator more times than I care to remember!

Because they realize this lack of discipline genuinely disturbs me, my children tried to help me with this nocturnal noshing.

One night I awoke and imagined a soft, sweet sound—similar to the siren song that sought to distract Odysseus—summoning me to the kitchen. Immediately, deep within, a warning voice cautioned that I was about to step onto the same old battleground. As I steathily slipped out of bed—exercising great care not to wake Rose—the voice reminded me I'd been wounded often before. But I was on the stairs now—the point of no return!

Approaching the refrigerator door, I sighted a note tacked upon it: "Should you really?" *Well,* I thought, *cute, but not convincing.* Reaching for the handle, I saw the second note: "Think twice." I did . . . just before I opened the door.

Even then, I knew it would be English muffins, a little bit of butter . . . about a quarter inch of peanut butter . . . then thirty seconds in the microwave. As my mouth began to water, I saw the note on the *unopened* muffins: "English muffins put pounds on." Unopened—if I even touched them, they'd know. So I closed the refrigerator, but the war wasn't over.

Next, the cookie cabinet. The door of that had a note,

too: "We're praying that you're losing." I opened it anyway, reaching for the double-filled Oreos, which are also
great dipped in peanut butter. That's when I saw the note
taped to the bag: "We love you." Dropping the bag like a
hot coal, I grabbed for the jar of peanuts. You guessed it—
another note—"We care." That's when I went back to bed!

I desperately want my children to lead ordered lives, and
I'd like to think we've prepared them to say no to things that
could erode their personal discipline. Before I do that, I
have to be a measured man . . . a disciplined daddy.

Only through the power of the Holy Spirit can I become
that!

Make It More

As you take those seven steps in parenting that teach
the essential lessons every child needs, make it even more
than that. Though we might look at the methods differently, neither you nor I can allow the opportunity to ex-
emplify faith for our children to pass us by. Both of us
need to commit ourselves to becoming an influence for
good . . . for a lifetime.

Make It Memorable

Chuck Swindoll tells a story about a daddy who planned
an exciting vacation with his family. On the day they were
scheduled to leave, he came home from the office and
reported he would not be able to accompany them as orig-
inally planned. Their faces registered deep disappointment. He insisted he could join them in a day or two, but
they wanted to wait—a couple of days didn't matter. This
was a family thing, and they didn't want to go without him.

Despite all the protests, he insisted they leave and saw
them off that afternoon. The station wagon was loaded up,
just packed for family fun, and their excitement returned as
he assured them he would join them as quickly as possible.
Watching them drive down the street, he had a hard time
concealing a smile. This was all part of *his* plan. . . .

He went inside . . . changed his clothes . . . and settled back to take things easy for a day or two—until the time was right. Because he had planned the vacation so carefully, he knew every road they would travel on. He knew exactly where he would join them.

He flew ahead to a distant city . . . had a driver take him to a particular point, past which he knew they would travel in a short time . . . then waited. Before long he sighted the family car in the distance. He picked up his bag, positioned himself by the side of the road, and stuck out his thumb like an ordinary hitchhiker. It wasn't a place where you'd normally find someone thumbing a ride; the family couldn't help but notice him as they sped by. Mom hit the brakes and backed up. Can you imagine the joy and laughter shared in the next moments? Dad just wanted to make sure they would never forget this vacation. It made it meaningful—he made it memorable.

Right now I'm doing a lot of things with my children that I hope will be just that. Years down the road, after I'm gone, I want them to remember the times we've shared. As they look back I'd like them to know I took every opportunity to invest in their lives.

Most of all, though, I'd like them to know I tried to model my faith in daily life. I want to make it memorable. And it will be, if only I take the opportunity before me now.

Make It Understandable

When Joshua led Israel across the Jordan, God commanded him to take twelve stones from the riverbed and build a monument to remind the people of the event. When later generations passed that crude altar, they would point to it and tell their children, "See, they were placed there by General Joshua, when God parted the river—at this very site—and brought us into the land of promise."

That altar held meaning for a whole people. God wanted them to remember He was still all He had ever been to

Israel. As He had graciously intervened in their lives before, He would again.

Moms and dads need to establish the same kind of altar.
If we take stones from our own lives and form an altar of
testimony, our children will point to it and understand its
meaning for their own lives.

Make It Enjoyable

Children learn better when they enjoy the process. Too
often, however, much of the spiritual input they receive is
unpalatable, because it's not relevant . . . and it's not enjoyable, because we shroud it in a solemnity that somehow makes God rather dull.

One night as our family shared after-dinner devotions,
one of the girls became a little bit giddy. I quietly gave her
one of those glances that normally does its work—but this
time it failed. Before long the second was fighting giggles
. . . then the third.

I stopped my reading to remind each that family devotions were a *serious* matter, but before I finished, Rose
began laughing as well. Indignant that they would abuse
a rather sacred time, I remember saying, "We are having
family devotions. It isn't a time for fun!"

That did it. A hush fell over the room . . . and I realized
what a dumb attitude I had. Why, this was meant as the best
time to enjoy life—delighting in God and the things He told
us about Himself and ourselves. I paused . . . looked at
Rose and the girls . . . and we all laughed heartily.

That night we made a commitment to enjoy our spiritual
times. It's okay to laugh . . . to clown . . . even when you
pray. . . . because you're saying "God, we enjoy this part
of life with You as fully as any other." Since then, devotion time hasn't been so dull in the Aker household. Often
we find it quite enjoyable!

Make It Venerable

Though we need to make it enjoyable, we can't take
times of our children's spiritual formation lightly. God's

mandate, which dates back to Abraham, is inviolable: "For I have chosen him, in order that he may command his children and his household after him to keep the way of the Lord by doing righteousness and justice; in order that the Lord may bring upon Abraham what He has spoken about him" (Genesis 18:19).

Parents—especially dads—need to understand that. If we are to fulfill God's plan and purpose for us, we must honor the fact that He has chosen and charged us to lead our children in their walk with Christ.

God gave Abraham a sacred commission, and He has given us one, too. He gives us the task of sharing pass-on-able truths. And that means modeling the message. On the Father's Day just before she left home for college, Laurie wrote a little piece entitled "Faces." It was her special gift to me. I want you to know up front that it's not all true—but I wish it were. Somehow I see it as Laura's gentle and loving reminder of what God wants me to be:

> Father—fishing on the riverbank . . . Teacher—helping me learn the Greek alphabet . . . Pastor—bringing me up in the way of the Lord . . . Husband—setting an example for your daughters . . . Learner—always willing to admit your mistakes . . . Disciplinarian—a firm velvet hand . . . Human—eight chocolate bars, two fishing poles, and a lot of fun . . . Worker—teaching me determination . . . Comedian—always bringing a smile . . . God fearer—on your knees in prayer . . . Comforter—answering my cry in the night . . . Supplier—always trying to make your family happy . . . Giver—always giving more, taking less . . . My friend and companion—taking time for little extras . . . Successful—your little girls' dad.

May you and your family become a "we" by sharing these truths and drawing closer to Him through them. His blessing on you all!

Six

Talking It Up

I have always loved animals; as a child I tried to smuggle puppies into our house. Unfortunately, Mom and Dad never fully shared my love for these cuddly creatures who cried at night . . . chewed the best furniture . . . and wet on the brand-new carpet.

Now that *I'm* the daddy, I have the pets I always wanted: My family and I breed, raise, and exhibit purebred golden retrievers. I've learned a lot about dogs—and people!

Many have commented on the uncanny likeness to their owners some dogs seem to have. In fact, each year a master-dog look-alike contest offers a grand prize of $10,000 to the best human-canine match. I'm willing to admit many physical similarities exist between people and dogs, but in our travels on the dog circuits, even more I've noticed that dogs and masters share a likeness of demeanor. People seem drawn by certain animals who share their characteristics.

You might even use the dog-master comparison in many Christians' approach toward witnessing. No, that's not as farfetched as you might think. Let me give you some examples. . . .

One type of witnessing Christian reminds me of a poodle. Have you noticed how this dog parades by with an elitist air? Somehow he gives you the impression he's the best in the canine world. He flaunts what he's got—just like some believers, who consider themselves above others and never stop to get close to people. As they prance by, you're sure they have *something*—but you're never sure just *what*.

Other Christians remind me of the collie. Basically a herding dog, the collie has a reputation as a tremendous fighter, who moves with lightning speed. I still remember Albert Payson Terhune's vivid descriptions of the collie in battle. A nip here, a lunge there, a grab for an ear—he's in and out quickly. Some Christians are like that with the gospel: a verse here, a tract there. They dart in and out with such speed that they're almost invisible, but they feel satisfied they've given you something.

The Airedale, the Ivy Leaguer of the canine world, reminds me of the absent-minded professor, a real intellectual. Some Christians know all the arguments and have all the answers. They can discuss anything from comparative religion to the finer points of escatology. But too often they become so preoccupied with the intellectual that they fail to observe the practical—that people in pain need comforting and touching.

Others remind me of the great Dane. This working dog is best known for his size, and even handlers of other breeds find his appearance quite intimidating. Some Christians come across like that, because they attack the unbeliever from a position of strength and appear flawless and without weakness.

The pit-bull terrier, commonly regarded as the fiercest of dogs, goes for the jugular—and never lets go. Encountering the pit bull is ever bloody. In some circles, well-intentioned people who long to see a believer come to Christ have made witnessing a bit like that. They've made up their minds that the non-Christian will receive the gospel . . . whether or not he wants it. Such witnessers go for the jugular and hang on. The path to their church is sometimes littered with the casualties of the pit-bull witnesser.

A less well-known dog, the basenji, is supposedly mute . . . the nonbarker of the dog world. He probably doesn't know he can be heard. When he communicates, it's in a language all his own. Some believers, like the basenji, don't know they can communicate their faith. When they try, too often they do it in a language all their own, with terms like *total depravity, the rapture, limited atonement, justification.* So many phrases that communicate precious little to the lost person get in the way of the message.

Finally we have the truly gracious canine, who does everything with class. Pardon my prejudice, but there *is* something special about the golden retriever. . . . He picks up with you at the beginning and stays by you to the end. He's known for his affection, gentle ways, and unending faithfulness.

Some of us need to be a bit more like the golden retriever. There are too many basenjis—silent . . . too many pit bulls—always out to win . . . too many great Danes— eager to intimidate . . . too many Airedales—all the facts and figures, but not a whole lot of relevance . . . too many collies—in and out ever so quickly, never staying around long enough to deal with the real issues . . . and too many poodles—flaunting a life-style, but never really sharing their lives.

Why does communicating the gospel present such a problem to the average Christian? Many remain shamefully silent, or fall into one of the traps I've mentioned already. Why do we hesitate? I'd like to suggest five reasons why the cat may have gotten our tongues.

We Lack Compulsion

Some Christians feel no compulsion to share the gospel with others and wonder, *Why should I tell people about Jesus?* From Jesus we have received the Great Commission: "Go therefore and make disciples of all the nations, baptizing them in the name of the Father and the Son and the Holy Spirit, teaching them to observe all that I commanded you; and lo, I am with you always, even to the end of the age"(Matthew 28:19, 20).

The Bible clearly teaches that *everyone* has sinned and is

separated from God (Romans 3:23); a tremendous gulf lies between God and man. Unequivocally, Jesus claimed He alone can bridge the gap: "I am the way, and the truth, and the life; no one comes to the Father, but through Me" (John 14:6). With that comes the parallel promise He made through Paul: "Whoever will call upon the name of the Lord will be saved. How then shall they call upon Him in whom they have not believed? And how shall they believe in Him whom they have not heard? . . ." (Romans 10:13, 14). Those who accept Him are saved, but their salvation depends on hearing the testimony of others who already believe. *We* are those witnesses.

Why do we communicate? Because we wish to obey the Master and we feel compassion for those who do not know Him.

How do we do it? Only by the power of the Holy Spirit, who enables us (as He enabled the apostles) to fulfill the Great Commission: "But you shall receive power when the Holy Spirit has come upon you; and you shall be My witnesses both in Jerusalem, and in all Judea and Samaria, and even to the remotest part of the earth" (Acts 1:8).

We Lack Confidence

Even though most Christians have heard the gospel over and over, few truly understand what makes up an evangelistic message. Just what are we to tell others?

Well, it's the *evangel,* the *gospel* . . . "good news." Many of us call ourselves *evangelicals,* because we've committed ourselves to communicating the evangel.

When the angels proclaimed the birth of Christ to the shepherds, they gave a total evangelistic message: "For today in the city of David there has been born for you a Savior, who is Christ the Lord" (Luke 2:11). Look at that again. "Today in the city of David there has been born" announces Christ. "For you a Savior" addresses our condition as sinners. Finally, that verse advocates commitment by identifying him as "Christ the Lord."

When Jesus calls us to come, it's not so that we can

party with Him. He beckons us to come and die. Remember, His path terminated at a cross—if you see it from an earthly perspective.

But the evangelistic message looks to an empty tomb. We follow not a crucified criminal, but a living Lord. In that great reality lies our confidence.

We Lack Conviction

Though we may believe Christ has commanded us to witness, we may not feel the task is ours. Most of the twentieth-century church seems quite content to leave the work of evangelism to more notable Christians. *After all, they may rationalize, Billy Graham has been preaching to hundreds of thousands for more than forty years. Bill Bright has led his crusade around the world. Even Bill Gothard has people leaving his seminars with a first-time assurance of salvation. What's left for me to do?*

God has always had His impressive messengers, but we are not excused from witnessing by a few men who have touched many lives. Though He communicated through prophets, angels, then Christ, He still says to each one of us: ". . . As the Father has sent Me, I also send you" (John 20:21).

Feeling must give way to fact. The task of messenger is ours!

Lack of Comprehension

At times believers evidence little comprehension of the process involved in a decision for Christ. Many have fallen for the idea that another's response to Christ is somehow up to us, but that is so wrong. We can only prayerfully, clearly, and gently present the truth; the decision rests with the individual.

As we understand that, we may feel liberated to tell the story more boldly. We cannot manipulate others. Sharing the gospel requires no gimmicks or high-pressure tactics. Never should we give the impression that we want to force someone's will to conform to ours. Jesus Christ has not fallen on His knees, crying, "Please accept Me, please accept Me." Rather He is seated on the throne in the heavenlies, and men and women must take Him as Lord.

How does that happen? when you and I, in the power of the Holy Spirit, share the story of God's love so that individuals are moved to place their trust in Christ alone.

We Lack a Construct

Finally, some—perhaps a majority—of evangelicals have absolutely no idea where to begin. Many cannot present the gospel in a logical fashion, because they do not have a handle on how to present Christ.

Peter advised the Christians scattered across Asia Minor, "Sanctify Christ as Lord in your hearts, always being ready to make a defense to everyone who asks you to give an account for the hope that is in you, yet with gentleness and reverence" (1 Peter 3:15). Clearly we have to be prepared to explain what we believe to others. We need a construct—a device that will take us through the salient points of the gospel.

There are so many to choose from. Christian bookstores carry many helpful pamphlets. But my own preference is "The Four Spiritual Laws." Obviously it is not the only one, or even the best, but it works for me. I keep a supply in my office and never travel without carrying a half dozen. Literally hundreds of times I have shared its truth with others and can recall only a few instances when they weren't moved by the clarity of this presentation.

Sharing the gospel is a difficult and demanding discipline. How much easier we find it to remain in the comfort zone of our holy huddle. But that's not what God has commanded us to do. If we wish to communicate the truth as He has called us to, we have to have compulsion . . . confidence . . . conviction . . . comprehension . . . and a construct—without them, no conversions!

A Person With a Procedure

Don't think I mean to imply that no one today ever witnesses. Faithful believers daily lead others to Christ at common yet crucial intersections of life.

The Person

One such intersection is recorded in Acts 8. In a situation uniquely orchestrated by the Holy Spirit, God used the deacon Philip in a powerful way.

In Samaria, Philip had started a great evangelistic thrust. Luke's record of its results makes it sound like a revival: "And the multitudes with one accord were giving attention to what was said by Philip, as they heard and saw the signs which he was performing. . . . And there was much rejoicing in that city" (Acts 8:6, 8).

At that crucial point in ministry, Philip became an unusual example of how God uses the right man at the right place, at the right time. God led him in an unexpected direction, and Philip had the *sensitivity* to respond. "But an angel of the Lord spoke to Philip saying, 'Arise and go south to the road that descends from Jerusalem to Gaza . . .' " (v. 26). Quite simply, "He arose and went . . ." (v. 27). We might have felt tempted to challenge God. After all, big things were happening in Samaria . . . people were being saved . . . Peter and John were in town . . . some got healed . . . others received the Holy Spirit . . . signs and wonders abounded. There was no lack of work there.

But God told Philip to head out for Gaza—and because the deacon was available to Him, he went. In the middle of the desert road, at about high noon, the pieces of God's plan began to fit together: "And behold, there was an Ethiopian eunuch, a court official of Candace, queen of the Ethiopians, who was in charge of all her treasure; and he had come to Jerusalem to worship. And he was returning and sitting in his chariot, and was reading the prophet Isaiah. And the Spirit said to Philip, 'Go up and join this chariot' " (vv. 27–29). Philip obeyed the Spirit's promptings, though such an influential man might have ridiculed and rejected him. But a person whom God can use has the special trait of *availability*. Philip willingly became God's man at the intersection.

The Procedure

Not only was Philip totally available to God, he also had a procedure—a method for communicating the gospel truth.

He had urgency. When the Spirit of God directed him to join the chariot, the Greek word picture suggests the deacon glued himself to the machine. The narrative continues, "And when Philip had run up . . ."; he didn't waste any time. God arranged that intersection, and Philip would not pass it by. The clock was running. So was Philip.

". . . He heard him reading Isaiah the prophet, and said, 'Do you understand what you are reading?' " (vv. 30, 31). That Philip *heard him* impresses me. The deacon listened. He didn't move in with his own agenda, by collaring that man and asking "Have you heard of 'The Four Spiritual Laws'?" He expressed genuine interest in what the Ethiopian was about. Philip comes across as a man of great authenticity. He cared about the Ethiopian and felt more committed to touching him in his area of need than imparting a specific body of truth.

Obviously moved by Philip's sincerity, the other man freely acknowledged he did not understand what Isaiah had written and asked Philip to explain it. Because the text was about the sacrificial Lamb, Philip ". . . preached Jesus to him" (v. 35). Avoiding tangential issues, Philip simply spoke about Jesus. Beginning in Isaiah and speaking of the man whom Micah prophesied would be born in Bethlehem . . . whom Zechariah predicted would be sold for thirty pieces of silver . . . whom David said would be nailed to a tree . . . he laid it all out. But he preached only Jesus.

A sense of urgency in communicating the gospel ought to mark our lives. Around my neck, I wear a dog tag that says:

> *John,*
> *Remember, I'll be back. . . .*
> *Jesus.*

I fully believe this could be at any moment. Somehow, I have to allow that to influence all my interactions with unsaved family and friends before time runs out.

When I communicate the gospel, I want my message to have Philip's sense of urgency, authenticity, and clarity. If I have only one chance to preach Christ to an individual or congregation, my message has to spring from deep within me and ring true to my listeners. I have neither time nor need for any message other than Jesus.

But as a preacher, I can easily fall prey to the lie that my evangelism is only or best done in the pulpit. One day in November, 1981, God drove home the truth that I am to seize every opportunity to tell all who will listen.

That Monday, on my way to a special meeting at Trinity College, in Deerfield, Illinois, I got a flight from Newark International Airport to Chicago's O'Hare.

I felt exhausted. The day before I had preached three morning services . . . taught a membership class at night . . . and preached an evening service. It was a down sort of day, when I took that flight.

As I boarded the DC-10, the emptiness of the flight surprised me. Many times I had traveled on it and found the plane quite full. Despite that, the computer had decreed I should sit beside a fellow traveler. He had the window seat . . . I had the aisle one. Looking across the five seats in the middle, I intended to lift the arms of all of them and stretch out. In the meantime, though I would be just a bit sociable—after all, I was a minister. So I began to speak with him.

His name was Dick, and I quickly found out we had much in common. We both had studied at the Army Intelligence School . . . had married women in army intelligence . . . and had three children. That's where our commonalities ended.

Dick told me he'd been to New York City's Sloan-Kettering Cancer Institute. He had come to an agreement with his doctors that there would be no more chemotherapy or radiation treatment. He just wanted to go home . . . back to Beatrice, Nebraska, where he worked as comptroller at the Lutheran hospital. He wanted to live full throttle before his kids. The doctors told him it would be just a few months—six, eight, maybe ten . . . but not many.

After a while, Dick began to turn toward me. Until then I had only seen the right side of his face—so normal . . . so whole. Little by little, the left side came into view, and I saw the ravages of the disease: basal cell carcinoma—"skin cancer." My father had had it, but on Dick it had run wild.

For the first time I saw the way the tongue lay in the mouth . . . how the teeth bit up and down into the jaw . . . the way the eye socket is formed and holds the eye in place—because all the skin was gone. It was one raw, open wound.

Here was a man facing certain death, short of a special miracle by God. Yet his greatest concern was for the three children he would have to leave behind. He told me he had been an only child, as was his wife. A few months earlier, she had fallen on the basement steps and died. Now as he knew he would have to leave his children, only his aged parents remained to care for them. They lived in New Jersey and had never known anything outside that state . . . and his children only knew Beatrice, Nebraska.

At that point I looked at Dick and asked, "Do you mind if I tell you why I'm not an intelligence agent anymore? Can I tell you about something that really changed my life?"

Dick nodded, and I took a napkin left over from breakfast and sketched out my version of "The Four Spiritual Laws." When I came to the end of that simple presentation, the stewardess interrupted our conversation: "We are now preparing for final descent into Chicago's O'Hare airport."

"Dick, can't you trust Jesus Christ for your future . . . what lies beyond the grave for you and your children? Can you look to the One who left His own grave behind and believe that He holds some hope for you and for the care of your children?"

Like a dying man, Dick clutched my hand and said, "Pray with me." Right then, at about ten thousand feet above Chicago, Dick Wieger gave his heart to Jesus Christ.

We had just concluded the sinner's prayer when the big plane touched down. Following Dick along the ramp and

into the lobby, I thought for a moment about my wife and
children. As we shook hands, I saw only the left side of
Dick's face. Thoughts of the suffering, sorrow, and separation before him burdened me. When I turned for one
last look, I saw Dick waving . . . only the right side of his
face, fully alive and warmly smiling, toward me. I reflected on the graciousness of God, who took someone
like me and allowed me to share in His work, the miracle
of taking people from death to life.

Had the story ended there, it would have remained
special. . . .

Within six weeks of that flight, I relocated to Deerfield
and assumed responsibilities as vice-president of Trinity
College. Part of my duties included a great deal of travel.

The first Sunday of May, 1982, I was on the East Coast,
preaching. Sunday seemed longer than before. Monday, I
got on the same flight to O'Hare, and felt tired . . . very
tired. But I was going home. The computer had graciously
reserved me a seat next to a nice older woman. I figured
she wouldn't mind if I sat back, buckled up, and went to
sleep, so I did just that. But shortly after breakfast I woke
up and realized I'd not taken time to invest in her life or
allowed her to share her life with me.

I began by asking if she lived in Chicago. No, she told
me. She was on her way to a little town in Nebraska. I
asked her which one.

"Oh, you've probably never heard of it," she warned me.

"Try me!"

"Beatrice."

"I know Beatrice," I responded. "I know the comptroller of the hospital there."

She looked at me in total surprise. "You know Dick?"

"Yes, I sat with him on this very plane last November
. . . this same flight."

"You must be John."

"How could you know that?"

She simply replied, "I'm Dick's mother."

June Wieger went on to tell me how Dick had begun to
walk in that decision he made for Christ. He was reading

the Bible . . . getting together with his pastor . . . praying
. . . concerned about Bible study. Having the assurance
that Dick was taking his final steps with his Master, with
her Lord, meant something special to June.

She also told me about her pain. Most mothers watch
their children grow and enjoy life, but she had to stand by
almost helplessly and watch her only son die. She expressed great concern that she and her husband, Rudy,
had never known anything outside New Jersey . . . and
the children had their roots in Nebraska. What was she to
do . . . ?

At this point the stewardess announced, "We're now
preparing for final descent into Chicago's O'Hare
airport."

Our eyes locked as I said, "You know, June, this is
when I prayed with Dick."

Just as her son had done, she took my hand and asked,
"Would you pray with me?" And I did.

The plane pulled up to the ramp just as we finished.
June looked at me and commented, "You know, I'm so
encouraged."

"Encouraged?" I replied. "I feel inspired! To think that
one casual meeting with Dick, and he's following through
on that decision . . . that he's been concerned about a
deeper relationship with his Lord . . . to see the way God
takes our lives, causes them to intersect, and puts all the
pieces together so perfectly . . . just the way He arranged
for us to sit together. People would never believe it."

She looked at me and said, "You know, this wasn't my
seat." We were in row twenty-six, seats A and B. "I was
assigned to row twenty-four, and just before you came on
board, a woman asked me to change seats with her."

I must confess I never find it easy to present the gospel
to a total stranger. I am a coward at heart. But the world is
filled with Dick Wiegers. I pray God will give me—and
you—the courage and grace to seek them out and communicate His love.

I look forward to seeing Dick Weiger again one day. . . .

Seven

_____ Elusive Worship

*E*very Sunday morning and on all the holy days of obligation Mom and Dad took us to Mass. The cathedral-like sanctuary awed me, but that emotion sprang from more than the building itself; the silence inside overwhelmed me. Both sanctuary and silence combined to prepare my heart to appreciate the majesty and mystery of the Godhead. Even as a child I understood this weekly excursion meant I had an encounter with God.

Entering Saint Joseph's Church, Mom and Dad walked with us, their three young children, down a long stone aisle. When we came to the pew Dad designated, each of us genuflected before the tabernacle, prominent on the high altar. Walking into the pew, we all made the sign of the cross, knelt, and began to prepare our minds and hearts for the mass. None of us dared move until Dad rose from his knees—that was our sign. Even as we sat back, we did so in absolute and sacred silence.

Before long, two altar boys, followed by the priest, entered the sanctuary. A bell rang, signifying that mass had begun, and as the altar boys and priest made their way to the front of the altar, we all rose. After a reverent pause, the priest genuflected while the altar boys and congregation knelt. Then we heard the familiar first words of that now almost forgotten Latin Rite: *"In nomine Patris, et Filii, et Spiritus Sancti, Amen.''* (In the name of the Father, and of the Son, and of the Holy Spirit, Amen.)*"Introibo ad altare Dei.* (I will go to the altar of God.)*"Ad Deum Qui laetificat juientutem meum.''*(To God who brings joy to my youth.)

I remember precious little about the sermons, except that they always seemed long; but one part of the Mass always thrilled me. Shortly after the priest washed his hands in preparation for the consecration of the bread and the wine, he would bow over the host—the small wafer he held in his hands—and recite: *"Hoc est enim Corpus Meum."* (For this is My Body.)

As he whispered the words of institution, he genuflected, elevated the host for all to see, placed it back on the altar, and genuflected again.

Then he took the cup into his hands and said: *Hic est enim calix Sanguinis Mei Qui pro vobis et pro multis effundetur in remissionem peccatorum.''* (And this is the chalice of My blood which shall be shed for you and for many for the forgiveness of sins.) After genuflecting once more, the priest raised the chalice high, placed it on the altar, and genuflected a last time.

A few moments later he turned, faced the congregation, held a small wafer above the gold ciborium and said: *"Ecce, Agnus Dei! Ecce, Qui tollit peccata mundi! Domine, non sum dignus . . . ut intres sub tectum meum, sed tantum dic verbum et sanabitur anima mea."* (Behold, the Lamb of God. Behold, He Who takes away the sins of the world. O Lord, I am not worthy . . . that Thou shouldst enter my dwelling, but only say the word and my soul shall be healed.)

Those words invited the faithful to come forward, kneel at the altar, and receive the Blessed Sacrament. As a young child I often felt left behind as my parents approached the communion rail without me. I longed for the day when I, too, would receive communion.

Occasionally I went to Mass with my grandfather and his brother. On those special times, when they approached the altar, they allowed me to walk between them. I still remember looking up at my grandfather, whom I loved so much, and seeing the tears streaming down his cheeks as he prepared for that sacred encounter.

Those experiences still linger in my mind, though they occurred more than forty years ago. Young though I may have been, they formed part of my spiritual journey and helped create within me a deep desire to experience God, to meet Him in those moments. Even then I had felt the pull of God's Spirit . . . His call to worship.

The Call to Worship

During my nine years in a monastery, my heart cry echoed the Psalmist's: "O God, Thou art my god; I shall seek Thee earnestly; My soul thirsts for Thee . . . in a dry and weary land where there is no water. Thus I have beheld Thee in the sanctuary, To see Thy power and Thy glory" (63:1, 2). Something impelled me toward God.

Though I never questioned the importance of worship during those years, its experience seemed to elude me, and I didn't really understand what worship was. Then came a time when the mystery and meaning vanished. Church merely became an expression of my religion, because I had become bound to a routine.

I'm not the only one who's ever felt that way. Peter Gillquist reflects the same feelings of elusive worship when he tells how some evangelicals wonder if they have missed out on something:

> A common complaint I hear over and over again is, "I just don't get anything out of worship." Often that statement is accompanied by another: "Our pastor is the best Bible teacher I have ever heard. When the man opens the Scriptures, I really learn. But our church has no sense of worship." There almost appears to be a pattern; the churches that are strongest on the preaching of the Scriptures are often the weakest when it comes to worshiping and giving praise to the Lord.

After I'd accepted Christ, the first time I ventured into a Protestant church, I expected the roof to suddenly split and a lightning bolt to dart from the heavens and strike me down in the pew. That Sunday I remember hearing the Word of God preached clearly, but I missed the awe of my childhood experiences.

Somehow, with the change of churches, I can't help feel that only the liturgy had altered. Whether or not we choose to admit it, Protestant churches have their own ritual—only evangelical ritual frequently proclaims the Word at the expense of appreciation of worship as an encounter.

Evangelical Protestantism ministers to my heart and mind, but those early days in the Catholic Church ministered to my soul. Somewhere one experience ought to bring all that together. Worship is more than incense and candles, but it also takes more than three points, a poem, and a prayer.

The Call From Scripture

Why do we seek this elusive thing? because God has placed the desire in our hearts, but also because Scripture calls us to worship. Although few congregations may have grasped worship's importance, we cannot blame that on the Word they proclaim. It's right there in the pages of the Bible.

Speaking through Moses in the Ten Commandments, God declared, "I am the Lord your God, who brought you out of the land of Egypt, out of the house of slavery. You shall have no other gods before Me. . . . You shall not worship them or serve them; for I, the Lord your God, am a jealous god . . ." (Exodus 20:2, 3, 5). He called us to worship Him and Him alone.

Commenting on the First Commandment, Martin Luther cited the following as transgressors of it:

> He who in his tribulation seeks the help of sorcery, black art, or witchcraft . . . .
> He who orders his life and work by lucky days, the signs of the zodiac and the advice of the fortune tellers . . .
> He who blames his misfortunes and tribulations on the devil or on wicked men, and does not accept them with

praise and love, as good and evil which come from God alone, and who does not ascribe them to God with thanksgiving and willing patience.

He who tempts God, and needlessly puts himself in dangers of body or soul.

He who glories in his piety, his wisdom, or other spiritual gifts. He who honors God and the saints only for the sake of temporal gain, and is forgetful of his soul's need.

He who does not trust in God at all times, and is not confident of God's mercy in all he does.

He who doubts concerning the faith or the grace of God.

He who does not keep back others from unbelief and doubt, and does not help them, so far as in him lies, to believe and trust in God's grace.

Here, too, belong all forms of unbelief, despair and misbelief.

Our worship calls us to affirm God by acknowledging in thought, word and deed that He is wholly other. We need to recognize Him as completely powerful in our lives.

The New Testament tells how Jesus was led out into the wilderness by the Spirit of God and there fasted forty days and forty nights. Afterwards, our enemy came to tempt Him. In the third temptation, the devil ". . . showed Him all the kingdoms of the world, and their glory, and he said to Him, 'All these things will I give You, if You fall down and worship me.' Then Jesus said to him, 'Begone, Satan! For it is written, 'You shall worship the Lord your God, and serve Him only' " (Matthew 4:8–10).

But what does it really mean to worship?

What Is Worship?

During seminary I learned to conduct weddings, funerals, baby dedications, and adult baptisms, but no one instructed me on how to lead people into worship. I suppose they assumed it would just follow naturally, but that isn't so. How we worship has a lot to do with our attitude toward God.

Focusing on Jesus

As I hungered for God in the monastery and later fell into a rather apathetic form of dutiful religion, I had not learned the lessons Luke teaches in the Book of Acts: Lordship dictates worship. Until He was Lord of my life, I could not worship Him. Instead of focusing on the founding of a religion, Luke set his sights on a reality that transformed. He concerned himself with a Savior . . . the Lord Jesus. If we would worship, we must begin there.

Once we understand who Jesus is, we fall at His feet, crying, "O Lord, I am not worthy!" Worship is the human response to divine revelation. Once I came to a fuller understanding of who Jesus Christ is, the desire that once filled my child's heart surfaced with even greater intensity. Now that I knew Him, I wanted to love and worship Him.

As I began to find answers in Scripture, specifically in the gospels, I saw how people encountered Jesus Christ and worshiped Him.

Seeing Jesus.   On the Mount of Transfiguration, Peter, James, and John stood awestruck as Jesus "was transfigured before them; and His face shone like the sun, and His garments became as white as light. And behold, Moses and Elijah appeared to them, talking with Him" (Matthew 17:2, 3).

Peter, you remember, wanted to build a place of worship right there. But before anything could be said or done about his proposal, the Father thundered from heaven, ". . . This is My beloved Son. . . ." When they heard that, the disciples fell on their faces, terrified. Once they dared look up, they saw only Jesus.

Worship means seeing Jesus and recognizing Him for who He is. It doesn't just happen, because we must make the effort to see Him.

Touching Jesus.   In another encounter with Jesus, a woman "who had had a hemorrhage for twelve years" interrupted and ". . . came up in the crowd behind Him, and touched his cloak. . . . And she . . . was healed of her affliction . . . (Mark 5:25–29).

We may see Jesus, but we also need to touch Him, to release His power. A church may have powerful preaching, an exciting choir, and a beautiful facility, but these helpful things alone will not create worship. Unless we recognize Jesus and reach out to Him, we cannot worship. Once we do that, we will never be the same.

Praising Jesus. In another gospel story, the triumphal entry of Jesus into Jerusalem, we see another dimension of worship. Luke tells us, ". . . the whole multitude of the disciples began to praise God joyfully with a loud voice for all the miracles which they had seen, saying, 'Blessed is the King who comes in the name of the Lord; Peace in heaven and glory in the highest!' " (19:37, 38).

Say what you will about the crowd that surrounded Him in the parade of palms, but never accuse them of lack of enthusiasm. They rejoiced in His presence . . . they celebrated God! They saw Him, some touched Him, but except for the self-righteous, who kept at a respectable distance, all became caught up in the grand celebration of Jesus.

How easily we get locked into certain patterns of worship behavior. Week after week we sit in our neat rows, folded hands, frozen faces, seemingly immovable. How unlike the Palm Sunday crowd, who had the freedom to express an inner impulse and rejoice in God. They danced, chanted psalms, leaped, waved, shouted, and spread branches before Him. They were fully caught up in their encounter with Jesus.

Enthusiasm makes a difference. Like any other great endeavor, worship requires our energies, not just our presence.

Once, while leading the Philadelphia Orchestra, Eugene Ormandy dislocated his shoulder. What they played doesn't really matter. He threw himself into his work so thoroughly, he did himself physical harm! That forces me to ask: *When was the last time I dislocated so much as a necktie in my enthusiasm for the Master?*

Approaching With Reverence

While we need enthusiasm in our worship, Scripture also admonishes us to do it decently and in order. Though we appreciate the role of the charismatic movement in returning warmth to a church bent on intellectualizing its faith, we walk on dangerous ground if we become so caught up in our familiarity with Him that we forget Jesus is God and His place is holy.

In one of his first public acts, Jesus drove the money changers from the temple. After pouring out their coins and overturning their tables, He commanded, "Take these things away; stop making My Father's house a house of merchandise" (John 2:13–17).

Let us not take God and His temple lightly; worship demands reverence for His purity and regard for His holiness. Both testaments clearly state, "You shall be holy, for I am holy" (1 Peter 1:16; *see* Leviticus 11:44). The very thought of His holiness ought to inspire us with a sense of awe that will characterize our individual and corporate worship.

"We are post-Reformation," we boast. We have done away with form without foundation. We have taken the body off the cross, we have moved the altar and removed the gold box, we no longer genuflect, and kneelers are a thing of the past.

These changes did not come easily for me, but I have come to accept them, because I realize none are essential. Yet it seems to me—as one who came to a saving faith in adulthood—that in breaking with the past we have diminished our concept of worship. Too often we forget to revere Him. We have made Jesus our Big Brother, and I'm not sure that's good theology. He is firstborn in a far different way from the one in which we are born of God. He is the Lord God, the Godman, and we cannot become casual about that.

Too much contemporary evangelism gives people the idea they can simply accept Jesus and live any way they want. We have not echoed His call to holiness: Churches are reluctant to demand it of their elders and deacons; in turn elders and deacons only reticently ask it of pastors. With that we have taken sin just a bit more lightly.

I see it in my own life. After all, now that I no longer practice or believe in auricular confession, I merely have to say, "God, I'm sorry." At one time I wrestled with a thorough examination of conscience before I entered the confessional and said, "Bless me, Father, for I have sinned," then enumerated to a fellowman my offenses before the Lord God of heaven. Perhaps I don't look at my life so thoroughly now because we've made the relationship seem quite safe.

In his *Chronicles of Narnia,* C. S. Lewis depicted our attitude so well. At one point the beavers try to picture the lion Aslan for Lucy, Susan, and Peter, strangers in the land of Narnia. The children feel excited and more than just a bit fearful about meeting him:

> "Ooh!" said Susan, "I'd thought he was a man. Is he—quite safe? I shall feel rather nervous about meeting a lion."
> "That you will, dearie, and no mistake," said Mrs. Beaver, "if there's anyone who can appear before Aslan without their knees knocking, they're either braver than most or else just silly."
> "Then he isn't safe," said Lucy.
> "Safe?" said Mr. Beaver. "Don't you hear what Mrs. Beaver tells you? Who said anything about safe? 'Course he isn't safe. But he's good. He's the King, I tell you."

Who ever said it was safe to come here before God? We should not take entering His presence lightly. When I say that I'm not speaking out of some old-time Catholicism or a message drawn from Jonathan Edwards. It comes from the caution of King David: "Who may ascend into the hill of the Lord? And who may stand in His holy place? He who has clean hands and a pure heart, Who has not lifted up his soul to falsehood, And has not sworn deceitfully" (Psalms 24:3, 4).

For me it has been a struggle to accept the somewhat lighthearted and flippant approach of evangelical corporate worship gatherings. Still I cannot accept the buzzing within the sanctuary, which takes place before the service—all in the name of fellowship. Nor can I accept the continual lateness of so many people who seem to wander in when the spirit—theirs—moves them.

If He is there as we come together, why would we talk to one another? If He meets us in a special way as two or three gather, why should we be late?

Perhaps I have more growth before me in this area. But I must confess that I find far more reverence for His purity in the high-church setting of my past than in the casual approach to worship that marks many evangelical congregations. Reverencing His purity is honoring our God.

Having a Right Heart

How do we properly worship this living and loving God? Part of the answer lies in these words of Jesus: "But an hour is coming, and now is, when the true worshipers shall worship the Father in spirit and truth; for such people the Father seeks to be His worshipers. God is Spirit; and those who worship Him must worship Him in spirit and truth" (John 4:23, 24).

Though I do not wish to depreciate the mandate of Hebrews 10:24, 25, which tells us not to forsake assembling together for worship, it takes more than just getting in one place. We also have to worship Him in spirit and in truth; we have to have a link with God.

That link starts with our hearts. We have to have:

Clean hearts
Yielded hearts
Focused hearts
Undivided hearts

To approach God, we must be right with Him. As David prayed, "Create in me a clean heart, O God, And renew a steadfast spirit within me" (Psalms 51:10).

We also need yielded hearts: "For who among men knows the thoughts of a man except the spirit of a man, which is in him? Even so, the thoughts of God no one knows except the Spirit of God" (1 Corinthians 2:11). In order to commune with God, we must know His thoughts. Our hearts must be yielded to His Spirit. Only when we withdraw from others for a time of prayer and meditation can we draw close to Him.

As an act of the will we need to focus our hearts on the Godhead. Ridding ourselves of the thoughts that distract us from Him is not easy—it takes discipline of the highest order—but without it we will not worship.

How often we can become sidetracked on a Sunday morning! The liturgy of the evangelical church may be little more than routine. We put our minds in neutral, allow our spirits to relax, and never really approach the throne of grace. The prophet Isaiah aptly described what God says of us then: ". . . This people draw near with their words And honor Me with their lip service, But they remove their hearts far from Me, And their reverence for Me consists of tradition learned by rote" (Isaiah 29:13).

Regardless of its beauty, we must not allow the rhythmic flow of religious routine to simply carry us along. Unless we focus our hearts on Him, we cannot worship.

Those who lead our worship services should be aware of the tendency of minds and hearts to stray and should orchestrate services to encourage our hearts to undivided worship. They need to ask, *Do announcements belong in the body of the service, or is worship better safeguarded if they are read beforehand? . . . Is the offering seen as a gift of self, continuing worship, or do people merely regard it as a halftime break? . . . . Does the movement up front resemble little more than a backfield shuffle?*

Several times Scripture refers to David as a man whose heart was wholly devoted to the Lord. Yet the Psalmist knew the distractions of his own humanity. At one point he cried out: "Teach me Thy way, O Lord; I will walk in Thy truth; Unite my heart to fear Thy name" (Psalms 86:11). How well the shepherd-king understood that worshiping the King of kings requires a heart that wills one thing . . . encountering the Living God.

Holding Faithfully to His Word

Ministry of music, reading of Scripture, time spent in private and public prayer—all these prepare the faithful for their heart-to-heart encounter with Christ. But Jesus said we must worship in spirit and in truth. If we put that together with the words he prayed the night before He was killed, "Sanctify them in the truth; Thy word is truth" (John 17:17), we can see we best worship God when we clearly understand His Word. The faithful application of His truth to our lives is most important. Everything before that point in public worship is our speaking to God, but through His message in Scripture, He speaks to us.

Many today would like to do away with serious study of God's Word as part of worship. I don't have a hard time understanding that desire: It's much easier to sit back and listen to a stirring testimony of one who has come to Christ . . . or the melodious strains of a gifted soloist. But when we give way to these lesser good things, our concept of God does not become properly informed and nurtured.

Our worship of God depends on our picture of Him. As A. W. Tozer wrote:

> The history of mankind will probably show that no people has ever risen above its religion, and man's spiritual history will positively demonstrate that no religion has ever been greater than its idea of God. Worship is pure or base, as the worshipper entertains high or low thoughts of God.
>
> For this reason, the gravest question before the Church is always God Himself. And the most portentous fact about any man is not what he at a given time may say or do, but what he in his deep heart conceives God to be. . . .

God's Word forms our conception of Him, and we cannot worship without the Word! Of this connection, John Stott has said:

> Word and worship belong indissolubly to each other. All worship is an intelligent and loving response to the reve-

lation of God, because it is the adoration of his Name. Therefore, acceptable worship is impossible without preaching. For preaching is making known the Name of the Lord, and worship is praising the Name of the Lord made known. Far from being an alien intrusion into worship, the reading and preaching of the word are actually indispensable to it. The two cannot be divorced. Indeed, it is their unnatural divorce which accounts for the low level of so much contemporary worship. Our worship is poor because our knowledge of God is poor, and our knowledge of God is poor because our preaching is poor. But when the Word of God is expounded in its fullness, and the congregation begin to glimpse the glory of the living God, they bow down in solemn awe and joyful wonder before His throne. It is preaching which accomplishes this, the proclamation of the Word of God in the power of the Spirit of God. That is why preaching is unique and irreplaceable.

True worship does not come easily to us. It requires uncommon discipline, but without such singlemindedness one deterrent will make worship impossible.

The Deterrent to Worship

We live in a day when the emphasis is totally on *me*. In our striving for possessions, position, power, and prestige, we worship success and seek the affirmation of the world.

When we buy into the world's standards like that, we become idolaters. James described it: "You adulteresses, do you not know that friendship with the world is hostility toward God? Therefore, whoever wishes to be a friend of the world makes himself an enemy of God" (James 4:4).

Even a casual flirtation with the world and its symbols of success, warns Job, places us under judgment:

> If I have put my confidence in gold, And call fine gold my trust, If I have gloated because my wealth was great, And because my hand had secured so much; If I have looked at the sun when it shone, Or the moon going in splendor, And my heart became secretly enticed, And my hand threw a kiss from my mouth, That too would have

been an iniquity calling for judgment, For I would have
denied God above.

Job 31:24–28

The altars to the lesser gods, which we construct within
our own lives, hinder worship. Too often we become more
impressed with our own petty empires than with the
Kingdom of God; then we reserve the best for ourselves
and God *may* get the residue.

Before long, self-interest spawns indifference to the Savior, as Charles Haddon Spurgeon showed:

> Why is it that some people are often in a place of wor-
> ship and yet they are not holy? It is because they neglect
> their closets. They love the wheat, but they do not grind it;
> they would have the corn, but they will not go forth into
> the field to gather it; the fruit hangs on the tree, but they
> will not pluck it; and the water flows at their feet, but they
> will not stoop to drink it.

Preoccupation with the temporal makes us lose track of
the eternal. Lured away from the Lord by our love for
lesser things, we fall prey to the trap C. S. Lewis's master
demon described to his nephew in *The Screwtape Letters:*

> Men have never known that ghastly luminosity, that
> stabbing and searing glare which makes the background of
> permanent pain to our lives. If you look into your patient's
> mind when he is praying, you will not find that. If you
> examine the object to which he is attending, you will find
> that it is a composite object containing many quite ridiculous
> ingredients . . . but whatever the nature of the composite
> object, you must keep him praying to it—to the thing that
> he has made, not to the person who has made him.

No matter the form it takes, the one deterrent to worship
is *self*—self-indulged . . . self-loved . . . self-enthroned.

Consequences of Worship

When we avoid the pitfalls that would keep us from true
worship, focusing our total beings on the presence of God,

we move from dull ritual to the unforgettable experience of divine reality. Such a heart-to-heart connection has several consequences.

God Is Exalted and Glorified

First, we will see God as God, recognizing that He is wholly other . . . above all else. Because He is the Awesome One, we exalt and glorify Him.

The Psalmist described it so beautifully:

> Let us come before His presence with thanksgiving; Let us shout joyfully to Him with psalms. For the Lord is a great God, And a great King above all gods, In whose hand are the depths of the earth; The peaks of the mountains are His also. The sea is His, for it was He who made it; and His hands formed the dry land. Come, let us worship and bow down; Let us kneel before the Lord our Maker. For He is our God And we are the people of His pasture, and the sheep of His hand.
>
> Psalms 95:2–7

We have an upward direction!

Saints Are Edified and Purified

True worship also has an inward dynamic: The saints are edified and purified. We can see it in the life of the Prophet Isaiah.

Shortly after the death of the prophet's good friend King Uzziah, Isaiah withdrew to the temple to be alone with God. He recollects the encounter:

> . . . I saw the Lord sitting on a throne, lofty and exalted, with the train of His robe filling the temple. Seraphim stood above Him, each having six wings; with two he covered his face, and with two he covered his feet, and with two he flew. And one called out to another and said, "Holy, Holy, Holy is the Lord of hosts, the whole earth is full of His glory." And the foundations of the thresholds

trembled at the voice of him who called out, while the temple was filling with smoke.

Isaiah 6:1–4

In the presence of God, Isaiah came to a deeper awareness of his sinfulness and cried out, "Woe is me, for I am ruined! Because I am a man of unclean lips, And I live among a people of unclean lips; For my eyes have seen the King, the Lord of hosts" (Isaiah 6:5). In response God directed one of the seraphim to take a burning coal from the altar and touch the prophet's mouth: ". . . Behold, this has touched your lips; and your iniquity is taken away, and your sin is forgiven" (Isaiah 6:7).

Silence filled the place, and Isaiah listened to all God said to him. Then he responded by leaving the temple, to become all God intended and do all He commanded.

Cleansed in that encounter with God, built up for the life and work before him, Isaiah could never be the same. His encounter with the Lord initiated recognition of his own need . . . was predicated on his retreat from the world and its noise . . . required respect for God's Word . . . and culminated in obedience.

Unless we encounter God in worship, when we go to church we have done little more than watch a stage play that made us feel good. If we do meet Him, we are moved to *be* good. Worship continues beyond the scope of an hour . . . beyond four hallowed walls.

When Jesus told Satan, ". . . You shall worship the Lord your God, and serve Him only" (Matthew 4:10), He linked worship with service. Confining it to the walls of a holy place does not answer; it must reach out to our daily lives and activities. If the holiness in the sanctuary does not become holiness in our lives, we have missed the point of worship entirely.

Sinners Are Evangelized and Persuaded

We have an upward direction and an inward dynamic but the saints' worship also has an outward dimension. As we cannot separate the Word and worship, so worship and witness become indivisible. If I have worshiped, my changed life ought to witness to those who do not walk closely with God. We can see that in the life of Moses:

> And it came about when Moses was coming down from Mount Sinai (and the two tablets of the testimony were in Moses' hand as he was coming down from the mountain), that Moses did not know that the skin of his face shone because of his speaking with Him. So when Aaron and all the sons of Israel saw Moses, behold, the skin of his face shone, and they were afraid to come near him.
>
> Exodus 34:29, 30

As he came off the mountain, the Israelites sensed something had happened to Moses. People should sense the same change in us, because genuine worship results in personal transformation. Through that change sinners are evangelized and persuaded. In 2 Corinthians Paul described the impact knowing Him has on our lives:

> For we are a fragrance of Christ to God among those who are being saved and among those who are perishing.
>
> 2 Corinthians 2:15

> But we all, with unveiled face beholding as in a mirror the glory of the Lord, are being transformed into the same image from glory to glory, just as from the Lord, the Spirit.
>
> 2 Corinthians 3:18

A skeptical watching world can see the difference. Renowned German philosopher Heinrich Heine challenges all who believe in Christ, "You show me your redeemed life and I might believe in your Redeemer."

Worship is the sacrament of encountering God and elevating Him. Through it God exercises our spirits and energizes our souls . . . eradicates our doubts and fears . . . enlightens our perspectives . . . and enhances our walk with Him. We see the evidence of the reality and sincerity of our worship in our fully renewed gift of self.

As we show renewed faith in our lives, we can unknowingly touch others, through our own reality and sincerity. My friend Bill Allison has written a sweet story based on the life of one man who touched him deeply. . . .

Jeremy was a grown man, but eternally a child. He was not equipped as you and I. He came into the world with the odds stacked against him. Those who knew Jeremy often saw him pedaling his bicycle all over town, with his prized possession, a little radio. He wore it strapped on his belt and its earphones ever in place. It represented his entire world. Only a few people in town knew his name—but almost everyone knew how special his radio was.

Day after day, Jeremy biked to the park, removed the headset, and rocked back and forth on the swings. As he did, he sang his own little song:

> *I swing high, I swing low*
> *But there's one thing that I know.*
> *I'm someone no one else can be.*
> *My name's Jeremy.*

Each Christmas a nativity scene was set up in the town square. It was simple—cardboard Joseph, cardboard wise men, and cardboard shepherds. Within the little wooden stable was the mother and her baby. During the Christmas season, the friendly but seemingly friendless Jeremy spent most of his time near the manger.

As people gathered one cold and snowy Christmas Eve, Jeremy was there among them. Many heard him say so softly: "I love the baby. I really love the baby." When he rode off in the snow, people noticed that by the manger Jeremy had placed his radio. He left it there—his gift . . . all he had.

They found him the next morning on a park bench. The Baby had taken both the gift and its giver.

Even though he might never have been able to define it, Jeremy knew the essence of worship. It means giving that which is most dear—all that we have, all that we are, and all that we do, to the One who is worthy.

Eight

_____ *In Hot Pursuit*

*D*espite his humanity—and at times his carnality—
he remains one of my heroes.

The humblest circumstances attended his birth: His father eked out a meager living as a miner, spending long,
laborious hours in the bowels of the earth; day after day
his mother foraged through the forests for twigs and
branches to fuel the kitchen stove—their only source of
heat. So impoverished was his family that no one could
have dreamed this young man would become a great
scholar and one day shake the theological and religious
foundations of the world. But he did. . . .

In 1505 young Martin, twenty-one years old, was a law
student at the University of Erfurt. Returning to school
after a visit with his family, he was caught in a sudden,
terrible, thunderstorm. Thoroughly frightened, Martin
darted for shelter beneath a nearby tree, but a bolt of
lightning struck him down in his tracks. In that awful
moment of near death—legend has it—for the first time
Martin Luther understood the holiness of God and his
own sinfulness. Seeking an intermediary between himself
and the inexorable Christ, Luther cried out: "Saint Anne,
help me! I will become a monk."

When the storm passed, the young man did not forget
his vow. Within two weeks Martin had put all his personal

affairs in order and, without the blessing of his father, applied for admission to an order of cloistered monks known as the Augustinians. Symbolic of the change in his life, Martin took *Augustine* as his religious name. After a year of rigorous monastic routine, Luther completed his novitiate and professed his vows as a monk. Two years later, Martin Luther was ordained to the priesthood.

But Luther still did not have peace with God. While he enjoyed the quiet and godly life of the monastery, each morning as he said Mass in one of the many monastery chapels he struggled deeply. His turmoil surfaced as he came to the first prayer at the offertory:

> *Suscipe, sancte Pater, omnipotens aeterne Deus, hanc imma-*
> *culatam hostiam, quam ego indignus famulus tuus offero tibi Deo*
> *meo, et vero, pro innumerabilibus peccatis, et offensionibus, et*
> *negligentiis meis, et pro omnibus circumstantibus, sed et pro*
> *omnibus fidelibus Christianis vivis atque defunctis: ut mihi, et*
> *illis proficiat ad salutem in vitam aeternam. Amen.*
>
> Receive, holy Father, omnipotent and eternal God, this spotless host, which I, your unworthy servant offer to You, my living and true God, for the innumerable sins, offenses, and omissions of both myself and these standing around, as also for all Christians—living and dead—so that this offering might profit these and myself with salvation in eternal life.

By the time the young priest approached the consecration of the Mass, his fears and confusion had reach a peak. He trembled as he took the wafer, then the cup, and whispered: *"Hoc est enim Corpus Meum. . . . Hic est enim calix Sanguinis Mei. . . ."* (For this is My Body. . . . This is the cup of My blood. . . .)

Luther dreaded the thought of addressing the One Living and True God before whom all men ought to tremble. In reflecting on his increasing sense of personal sinfulness and unworthiness, he later wrote: "I am dust and ashes and full of sin. . . ."

It seemed the more Luther tried to draw near to God,

the more His holiness filled him with terror. Despite his commitment to the ascetic practices of monasticism and the sacramental life of the church, Luther felt no closer to God. In fact, the conviction that he could not satisfy God at any point overwhelmed him.

In the several years that followed, Luther's order chose the troubled Augustinian to represent them at a hearing in Rome. Unfortunately, the immorality and indifference so prevalent there among churchmen further alienated him. Upon returning from the Holy City, Luther was reassigned to the Augustinian community in Wittenberg. Here his search for reconciliation with God brought him through a period of mysticism, into his personal study of Scripture.

In 1513, Luther began his explanation and exposition of the Psalms. In the fall of 1515, he entered Paul's letter to the Romans. Through that study Luther experienced reconciliation and embarked on his own personal relationship with the God for whom he had so long sought. Of that study he later wrote:

> I greatly longed to understand Paul's Epistle to the Romans and nothing stood in the way but that one expression, "the justice of God," because I took it to mean that justice whereby God is just and deals justly in punishing the unjust. My situation was that, although an impeccable monk, I stood before God as a sinner troubled in conscience, and I had no confidence that my merit would assuage him. Therefore I did not love a just and angry God, but rather hated and murmured against him. Yet I clung to the dear Paul and had a great yearning to know what he meant.
>
> Night and day I pondered until I saw the connection between the justice of God and the statement that "the just shall live by his faith." Then I grasped that the justice of God is that righteousness by which through grace and sheer mercy God justifies us through faith. Thereupon I felt myself to be reborn and to have gone through open doors into paradise. The whole of Scripture took on a new meaning, and whereas before the "justice of God" had filled me with hate, now it became to me inexpressibly

sweet in greater love. This passage of Paul became to me a gate to heaven. . . .

If you have a true faith that Christ is your Savior, then at once you have a gracious God, for faith leads you in and opens up God's heart and will, that you should see pure grace and overflowing love. This it is to behold God in faith that you should look upon his fatherly, friendly heart, in which there is no anger nor ungraciousness. He who sees God as angry does not see him rightly but looks only on a curtain, as if a dark cloud had been drawn across his face.

Although the day and the way differ greatly, I nonetheless identify with Luther in his quest for a relationship with the Godhead. . . .

Neither a thunderstorm nor the intercession of Saint Anne directed my path ultimately to the Passionist Fathers. Rather, it was a stormy preadolescence that prompted Mom one day to literally take me by the ear to the rectory at Holy Family Parish in Hicksville, Long Island.

As we sat in the small parlor, the minutes seemed to drag on into hours. Although Mom looked quite peaceful, I knew I had pushed her beyond her limits. Inside I knew she was deeply hurt and more than just a little concerned about this middle child. As for me, I was scared to death. I could not believe she was going to subject either one of us to this. Yet I should have known better. When Mom said she was going to do something, she usually followed through. . . .

She had given me fair warning. She told me just one more outburst—one more bad report from school . . . one more incident at home—and she would take me right over to the rectory and have me straightened out. When we got there, she did not simply ask to see one of the priests. Mom had a way of going to the top! She asked to see the pastor, Father Martin O'Dea.

She could have asked for Father Fagan—he was a teddy bear, a soft, gentle man. Or maybe the new priest—he looked as if he was just out of seminary. But Father O'Dea looked so stern that he had the shortest line outside his confessional booth on Saturday evenings. Even the adults tried to steer clear of him. Before long I heard footsteps approaching the parlor. The door opened. It was the young priest. . . .

"I'm Father Buckley," he said. "Harold Buckley." Mom stood up, shook his hand, smiled at him, pointed to me and began: "His name is John. He's Catholic. His father and I have tried everything we know. Now it's your turn!"

Poor guy didn't even know what to expect! But after inviting us to sit down, he looked at me and said softly: "Tell me what this is all about, John. . . ."

I would rather have told him so many other things—shameful though they might have been: that I was running with the wrong crowd . . . had been stealing from a neighbor's home . . . vandalizing public property . . . stripping bicycles at the high school . . . had been caught smoking (in the church bathroom!) . . . had been repeatedly thrown out of math class . . . and had even begun cutting Mass on Sunday.

But this was worse. I really did not want to get into this with him or anyone else. Almost thirty-five years later, it remains one of my most painful memories. Should I live to be a hundred, I'll never forget how badly I hurt Mom that day. I had just been caught again in another of my many untruths. When Mom asked me to explain my actions, I looked at her sneeringly and said: "Drop dead!"

Just about then, Father Buckley suggested that Mom wait in another room. I do not remember all that transpired. But this I do know: In those first few moments alone with this young curate, he convinced me that he truly cared about me and that although what I had done was terribly wrong, he would try to help me make it right. Despite the shame threatening to swallow me up, he put his arms around me . . . and somehow I began to feel whole.

I was twelve years old, just entering the eighth grade. The preceding year had been a veritable disaster. In the course of four quarters I had successfully managed to fail each of my subjects—including gym—at least once. I carried forward into that new academic year the reputation for being a tough guy . . . a do-nothing goof-off . . . a wiseacre. But even as we left the rectory that afternoon, I knew things were going to be different. . . .

They soon were. The more this young priest opened himself to me, the more I wanted to be with him. Before long my friends began to change . . . and my language . . . my habits . . . the way I dressed . . . even my free-time pursuits. By year's end, I was an altar boy, attended Mass and received communion daily, and was an honor-roll student at school. Even my teachers admitted—though somewhat skeptically—*something* had happened.

That something was no secret to me: Father Buckley's love for me was so genuine. Even more, in it I saw something of his love for Christ. It permeated his whole person—it was the magnet to which I was drawn. I wanted to know that kind of life. Because I could not *be* Father Buckley, I wanted to be *like* Father Buckley. That's when I realized I wanted to be a priest. . . .

That decision eventually led me to Cathedral College of the Immaculate Conception, the preparatory seminary for the Diocese of Brooklyn. During this period of study, I read and reread Butler's *Lives of the Saints*. That work, along with Thomas a Kempis's *The Imitation of Christ*, awakened within me a deeper appreciation for the great men and women who chose to express—or felt called to express—their love and commitment to Christ through lives of penance and self-denial behind cloistered walls. Somehow living—even as a priest—in this world was no longer attractive to me. I wanted to follow Christ more closely . . . without the weight of the world dragging me down or holding me back.

After two years at Cathedral, I was accepted as a postulant with the Passionist Fathers. The Passionists were a semicontemplative congregation of priests and brothers whose apostolate (ministry) was both contemplative (a life of prayer within the monastery) and active (preaching renewal through the Passion of Christ in the local parishes). Upon completing four years of postulancy at Holy Cross Seminary in Dunkirk, New York, I was accepted as a novice and began my novitiate at Saint Paul's Monastery in Pittsburgh, Pennsylvania. A little more than a year

later, I professed my vows as Confrater André of Our
Lady of the Holy Cross. I was a monk.

Along with my classmates, I was transferred to Holy
Family Monastery in Hartford, Connecticut, where we
continued our preparation for the priesthood in a classic
scholastic tradition, with a strong emphasis on spiritual
formation.

We were privileged to have as our director of student
life, a devout young Passionist, Norbert Dorsey. He became both friend and father confessor to me and stood
with me in some of the fiercest spiritual struggles I have
known—the greatest of which centered on whether I
should continue in the religious life or return home. That
decision did not come easily. Only Norbert's blessing enabled me to leave the monastery without feeling I had
abandoned God's will for my life.

Upon returning home, I completed my degree at Saint
John's University, in Jamaica, New York. Unsure about
what the future held for me, I entered the United States
Army. My tour with an intelligence unit in Washington,
D. C., saw me drift further away from the ideals I once
cherished as a young monk. During the years that followed I knew times of inner turmoil and guilt. So my
search intensified. Only then did I realize that my
allegiance—I cannot speak for others—but *my* allegiance
was to the church . . . not the Lord of the church.

Although I continued to be very active in our local
church, I sensed that I was not at peace with God . . . or
myself . . . nor *anyone*, for that matter. Then through the
ministry of Ned and Margaret Thomas, Mom and Dad,
and my lovely wife, Rose, I was shown on the pages of
Scripture that without Christ, I was lost and would be
separated from God forever.

Not in Paul's epistle to the Romans, but through his
letter to the Ephesians, I came to understand that I had
really been relying on my own works, my own efforts, to
make peace with a holy God—and all in vain. The text was
so clear: "For by grace you have been saved through faith;
and that not of yourselves, it is the gift of God; not as a
result of works, that no one should boast" (Ephesians 2:8,

9). I identify so fully with Luther at that point: "Thereupon I felt myself to be reborn and to have gone through open doors into paradise. . . ."

A new life had begun. I experienced what it meant to be a new creature. It's difficult to believe that was almost two decades ago. . . .

In the years since that initial commitment, I've learned I cannot allow my Christian life to rest solely on a decision made March 30, 1968. In fact, discipleship is not a once-for-all event, but an on-going experience with the Master. It is saying yes to Him day after day after day. For too long I had confused the ritual and routine of my life as a Catholic with the reality of being in Christ.

Evangelicals, too, fall into that way of thinking, so I believe the church today needs to rethink discipleship. For the most part, we use *discipleship* to describe a relationship in which one person imparts certain truths about Christ to another, while striving to influence that person with the quality of his own life. Though this is one aspect, it is at best secondary! More, if we are not careful, that very emphasis can overshadow and ultimately deprive us of the Real.

Discipleship is not a program of instruction . . . a doctrinal system . . . or an abstract Christology. It is not *about* Christ—discipleship *is* Christ. Nothing less than adherence to Jesus Christ and exclusive attachment to His Person will do. Discipleship must first involve intimacy with the Master and will certainly include imitation of His life and immersion in His teaching. It is Christ—the beginning . . . the center . . . and the end of life.

Even as I write that, I struggle deep within over what being a Christian means. I remain absolutely convinced that discipleship is not a supposed second step in Christianity. We ought to see it not so much as an invitation of the Master, but as an imperative!

The Path to Discipleship

The songwriter poses a powerful question: "Must I be carried to the skies on flowery beds of ease?" Well, if the truth were known, at times I would have to respond in the

144 Lengthen Your Stride

affirmative. If there were an easy way to get to heaven, I'd choose it. But that road does not exist. What does make up the path described by the ministry of Jesus?

Severance. In order to be His disciples, Jesus calls us away from our former ways of life. Leaving Nazareth, after healing a paralytic: ". . . He saw a man, called Matthew, sitting in the tax office; and He said to him, 'Follow Me!' And he rose, and followed Him" (Matthew 9:9).

Jesus' "Follow Me" is an imperative, not an invitation, and He used it thirteen times in Scripture. In response to this stark command, Matthew had two options: He could stay right where he was . . . or he could leave it all and follow. If he did as Jesus commanded, his life would never be the same. Dietrich Bonhoeffer described the alternatives:

> The first step, which follows the call, cuts the disciple off from his previous existence. The call to follow at once produces a new situation. To stay in the old situation makes discipleship impossible. Levi must leave the receipt of customs and Peter his nets in order to follow Jesus. . . . The call to follow implies that there is only one way of believing on Jesus Christ, and that is by leaving all and going with the incarnate Son of God.

If we would be disciples, we have to respond to the same call. Our lives, too, will never be the same.

Repentance. Severing ourselves from a former life-style is not enough to make us disciples. We must also have a radical change of mind called repentance:

> And after John had been taken into custody, Jesus came into Galilee preaching the gospel of God, and saying: "The time is fulfilled, and the kingdom of God is at hand; repent and believe in the gospel." And as He was going along by the Sea of Galilee, He saw Simon and Andrew, the brother of Simon, casting a net in the sea; for they were fishermen. And Jesus said to them, 'Follow Me. . . .'"

Mark 1:14–17

Before calling Simon and Andrew, Jesus calls them to repent. Like them, we need to look back over our old lives and say: *I don't want that anymore. . . . I reject that bitterness. . . . I will no longer be party to gossip. . . . I will not give impurity access to my mind. . . . I will not be partner in an adulterous relationship. . . . I will not settle for second best. . . . I don't want religion—I want the reality of Jesus Christ. I changed my mind, . . . and I hereby turn my back on yesterday.*
Only then can we become disciples!

Obedience. As His disciples God calls us to hear, study, and know the Word of God, but He does not end there. We also must submit to its authority and fulfill it. Jesus makes it abundantly clear that without obedience, no lordship exists:

> And why do you call Me, "Lord, Lord," and do not do what I say? Everyone who comes to Me, and hears My words, and acts upon them, I will show you whom he is like: he is like a man building a house, who dug deep and laid a foundation upon the rock; and when a flood rose, the river burst against that house and could not shake it, because it had been well built. But the one who has heard, and has not acted accordingly, is like a man who built a house upon the ground without any foundation; and the river burst against it and immediately it collapsed, and the ruin of that house was great.
>
> Luke 6:46–49

He leaves us no room to pick and choose the places in which we'd like to follow Him; instead He requires all of us. Though we need not know all the truth immediately— we do not immediately become perfect—once His Spirit makes us aware of the truth, He expects us to embrace it . . . and live it!

Perseverance. Staying alive in Christ means we feed on Him: ". . . Truly, truly, I say to you, unless you eat the flesh of the Son of Man and drink His blood, you have no life in

yourselves" (John 6:53). In telling the Jews that, Jesus
meant that if they wanted to get beyond the hypocrisy of
religion, they needed to feed on Him—and Him alone.

Many of us do not grow . . . do not know joy . . .
cannot rise above circumstances . . . cannot release the
things of this world, because we do not feed on Jesus. We
satisfy lesser appetites, but fail to taste of Him.

Then, as now, that demand was a big one, and shortly
after Jesus told them to feed on Him ". . . many of His
disciples withdrew, and were not walking with Him any
more" (John 6:66). As they left, Jesus turned to the twelve
and asked if they would also leave. Simon, their spokes-
man, showed their perseverance when he answered:
". . . Lord, to whom shall we go? You have words of
eternal life. And we have believed and have come to know
that You are the Holy One of God" (John 6:68, 69). No
turning back for that intimate band. Of this *stuff* God
makes disciples.

Significance. Not only does Jesus' call to discipleship
bring us closer to Him, it binds us to one another. Let's do
away with the destructive minority mentality that cripples
so many evangelicals!

Jesus has not called us to become part of a great institution we can take pride in . . . some successful business
venture in which we have a share . . . or a worldwide
organization we can belong to. No, He has called us to a
task of eternal significance: the building of His church.
"And I also say to you that you are Peter, and upon this
rock I will build My church; and the gates of Hades shall
not overpower it" (Matthew 16:18). The commission to
Peter extends to us, too.

Diligence. To succeed in this mission—and remember,
He has not called us to failure—we must willingly apply
ourselves to the task at hand. We must get on with it, even
if we must go it alone.

One man lacked the single-minded focus it takes to be
His disciple: "I will follow You, Lord; but first permit me
to say good-bye to those at home," he excused himself.

Jesus could not accept that: "But Jesus said to him, 'No one, after putting his hand to the plow and looking back, is fit for the kingdom of God' " (Luke 9:61, 62).

None of us can turn back from our appointed road. Discipleship requires more of us.

The Price of Discipleship

When we embark upon it, we will find discipleship a costly endeavor. Yet too much contemporary evangelism allows people to believe they need only say yes to Jesus at the end of a brief presentation of spiritual truth. Rarely will we tell the full story of both costs—Jesus' and the one we, too, must pay.

More than a hundred years ago, Bishop J. C. Ryle addressed the cheapness of much faith:

> Very likely [your religion] costs you nothing. Very probably it neither costs you trouble, nor time, nor thought, nor care, nor pains, nor reading, nor praying, nor self-denial, nor conflict, nor working, nor labor of any kind. . . . Such a religion as this will never save your soul. It will never give you peace while you live, nor hope while you die. It will not support you in the day of affliction, nor cheer you in the hour of death. A religion which costs nothing is worth nothing. Awake before it is too late. Awake and repent. Awake and be converted. Awake and believe. Awake and pray. Rest not till you can give a satisfactory answer to my question, "What does it cost?"

What does it cost to follow Jesus? Ten percent of my pay? wrong! A few hours a week in church? wrong! The price of being a disciple is nothing less than a life fully yielded to Him.

The wealthy Count Zinzendorf became captivated by a simple yet powerful painting of the suffering Christ. Something about the work clearly indicated the artist knew the anguish of Jesus. Beneath the painting, on a small metal plate, were engraved the words: "All this I have done for you. . . . What will you do for Me?"

Many would have responded with a solemn nod, little more than a thoughtful pause. For Zinzendorf that short message went to the core of his being. What would he do for Christ? He renounced all the world had to offer . . . enthroned Christ truly as his Lord . . . and began one of the largest missionary movements ever known.

Absolute austerity.   Jesus gave us a very clear picture of what it costs us to follow Him. The price is dear:

> If anyone comes to Me, and does not hate his own father and mother and wife and children and brothers and sisters, yes and even his own life, he cannot be My disciple. Whoever does not carry his own cross and come after Me cannot be My disciple. . . . So therefore, no one of you can be My disciple who does not give up all his own possessions.
>
> Luke 14:26, 27, 33

We cannot take such harsh statements lightly or try to alter the call issued by the Master. Unless our love for family seems like hatred, compared to our love for Him, unless we take up a cross, unless we surrender our ownership of everything, we have not become disciples.

Nor can we try to see this as an isolated teaching incident in the Master's life—He never meant it for a select few. "And He was saying to them all, 'If anyone wishes to come after Me, let him deny himself, and take up his cross daily, and follow Me. For whoever wishes to save his life shall lose it, but whoever loses his life for My sake, he is the one who will save it. For what is a man profited if he gains the whole world, and loses or forfeits himself?' " (Luke 9:23–25).

Return with me to that Scripture. Don't pass over it quickly or try to explain it away. Following Christ means saying a radical no to self—day by day . . . moment by moment—in order to embrace Christ and the Christ life. We cannot eradicate the meaning of those words. Discipleship speaks of an absolute austerity that can only be accepted (and even then with great difficulty) by those completely rewired within . . . made over . . . born again.

Human hostility. Those who take Christ's imperatives seriously will immediately and inevitably be out of step with those about them . . . not merely in the world, but in the church as well. High-minded seriousness about discipleship too often encounters human hostility. Jesus warned us:

> If the world hates you, you know that it has hated Me before it hated you. If you were of the world, the world would love its own; but because you are not of the world, but I chose you out of the world, therefore the world hates you. Remember the word that I said to you, "A slave is not greater than his master." If they persecuted Me, they will also persecute you. . . .
>
> John 15:18–20

When we commit ourselves to the strenuous task of discipleship, some in our families may regard us as strange . . . others will feel intimidated . . . some in the church may not want to associate with us any longer. Bishop Ryle comments:

> A man . . . must be content to be thought ill of by man if he pleases God. He must count it no strange thing to be mocked, ridiculed, slandered, persecuted and even hated. He must not be surprised to find his opinions and practices in religion despised and held up to scorn. He must submit to be thought by many a fool, an enthusiast and a fanatic— to have his words perverted and his actions misrepresented. In fact, he must not marvel if some call him mad. . . . To be a Christian will cost a man the favor of the world.

Yet to such divine madness the Christ calls us. Will we turn Him down?

Satanic strategy. If we can pass by the influence of those who would make us just like them, we still must deal with the enemy himself. It is all part of the price of discipleship.

Just as He warned of the hatred of men for His disciples, Jesus warns us that Satan will try every strategy that neutralizes or minimizes a serious commitment to discipleship.

Peter, the impetuous and impulsive leader of the twelve, often boasted of his love's constancy and declared he would never abandon the Master. Jesus knew that wasn't so and tried to prepare Peter for the enemy's onslaught: "Simon, Simon, behold, Satan has demanded permission to sift you like wheat" (Luke 22:31). To me it seems Jesus was really saying: "Peter, I love you . . . and I know you love Me. But Satan wants to destroy you. He has sought the Father's permission to tempt you any way he can. Peter—the Father has granted that request. Brace yourself, My friend, because the enemy hates you and will try this very night to destroy you."

Not only did Jesus know Peter would weaken, He knew the disciple would no longer feel the kingdom had a place for him and would return to his boat, nets, and the sea. But Jesus would also meet him on the shore and call him again to Himself.

The devil wants us to fail and buy the lie that we cannot be restored; it's all part of his strategy.

Early on in my military career, a friend of mine with Campus Crusade for Christ arranged a breakfast for myself, him, and Colonel Jack Fain—then coordinator of Campus Crusade's military ministry. At the end of breakfast, Colonel Fain reached across the table, grabbed my hand, and said: "Captain, remember—the devil hates you and has a diabolical plan for your life. . . ."

Jesus said it . . . Colonel Fain repeated it . . . and I really believe it. Satan would like nothing better than to discredit my life and thus destroy my ministry. He wants to tear through me like a windstorm. Sometimes, his wiles are easily detected. Other times his lure is far more subtle. Even as I pen these words, I hear echoing in my memory the warning chanted each evening in the monastery as the monks gathered for Compline—the last Hour of the Divine Office: *"Fratres, sobrii estote et vigilate quia adversarius vester diabolus tamquam leo rugiens circuit quaerens quem de-voret. Cui resistite fortes in fide. . . ."* Although I understood its meaning then, I never noticed its source. It is found in 1 Peter 5:8 (TRANSLATION MINE): "My brothers, be serious minded and vigilant because your enemy, the devil, goes about like a roaring lion seeking whom he might devour. Be strong in faith, resist him. . . ."

We need not give in to Satan's temptations. Instead, we can hold on to the truths of God and become powerful disciples for Him. To do that, we'll have to beware of his attacks from the outside—and within.

Internal Discipleship Perils

Not only do we face the perils of people, who would have us conform to their life-styles and Satan, in our personal journey with Jesus, we can encounter internal perils.

Egotism. Our greatest enemy in the spiritual life is often self, as is illustrated by a conversation Jesus had with the twelve:

> And an argument arose among them as to which of them might be the greatest. But Jesus, knowing what they were thinking in their heart, took a child and stood him by His side, and said to them, "Whoever receives this child in My name receives Me; and whoever receives Me receives Him who sent Me; for he who is least among you, this is the one who is great."
>
> Luke 9:46–48

Jesus knew their thoughts—as He knows ours. They were preoccupied with self . . . prestige . . . position . . . prominence. Their conversation sounded like a distant echo of Lucifer's words: ". . . I will ascend to heaven; I will raise my throne above the stars of God, And I will sit on the mount of assembly In the recesses of the north. I will ascend above the heights of the clouds; I will make myself like the Most High" (Isaiah 14:13, 14).

Although He tried to point out that the world's standards for greatest and least were not His, the twelve never really got Jesus' message. Again the same discussion surfaced as they sat in the Upper Room, just before His betrayal: "And there arose also a dispute among them as to which one of them was regarded to be greatest" (Luke 22:24).

How could they have missed it? we wonder. Only moments before, the Master had wrapped a towel about His waist, took a pitcher and basin, and washed the feet of those same men. Yet here they were, arguing about their places in the kingdom!

We need to look at our own lives and find the same attitudes we need to eradicate. If we would really follow Him, we must make Paul's *Carmen Christi* (Song of Christ) our own:

> Have this attitude in yourselves which was also in Christ Jesus, who, although He existed in the form of God, did not regard equality with God a thing to be grasped, but emptied Himself, taking the form of a bond-servant, and being made in the likeness of men, And being found in appearance as a man, He humbled Himself by becoming obedient to the point of death, even death on a cross.

> Philippians 2:5–8

With that outlook on life, we become effective disciples.

Materialism. As Jesus walked along a beaten path, pressed by would-be disciples, He pointed out another deterrent to discipleship: "And as they were going along the road, someone said to Him 'I will follow You wherever You go.' And Jesus said to him, 'The foxes have holes, and the birds of the air have nests, but the Son of Man has nowhere to lay His head' " (Luke 9:57, 58).

The beauty and simplicity of Jesus' life drew people. Had I walked side by side with Him on that dusty road, I, too, might have enthusiastically claimed, "Wherever You go, I will go." But I'm afraid He would have spoken to me as He did that individual. In essence, He told this would-be follower: "There's not much to be gained in this world by following Me. I own none of its goods. Even the animals do better than I—at least they have a home. I have none."

Jesus had a passion not for material things, but for men and women. As He proclaimed in the Sermon on the Mount, we have a clearcut choice: God or Mammon . . . we cannot serve both. At times, because we easily become seduced by the lure of lesser gods, our world seems one great materialistic temple.

Scripture warns us: "Do not love the world, nor the things in the world. If anyone loves the world, the love of the Father is not in him. For all that is in the world, the lust of the flesh and the lust of the eyes and the boastful pride of life, is not from the Father, but is from the world" (1 John 2:15, 16). Could it have been spelled out more clearly? The lust of the flesh . . . the lust of the eyes . . . and the boastful pride of life. We see something . . . because it looks good we want it . . . and because we want it, we take it. Those same steps were a part of the fall: "When the woman saw that the tree was good for food, and that it was a delight to the eyes, and that the tree was desirable to make one wise, she took from its fruit and ate; and she gave also to her husband with her, and he ate" (Genesis 3:6). Eve saw it . . . it delighted her because it appealed to her pride . . . and she took it.

The world knows our weakness and wraps the package so we find it irresistible. What begins as a seemingly innocent act can end in spiritual ruin. Maybe it begins with our becoming a bit too careless about our involvement with the world. We forget James's warning: "You adulteresses, do you not know that friendship with the world is hostility toward God? Therefore whoever wishes to be a friend of the world makes himself an enemy of God" (James 4:4).

Continuing in our own way, we become contaminated by the world. Instead of living with the kind of purity of life he prescribes, "This is pure and undefiled religion in the sight of our God and Father, to visit orphans and widows in their distress, and to keep oneself unstained by the world" (James 1:27), we begin to live as the world does and become almost numb to its attempt to conform us to its image and likeness: "And do not be conformed to this world, but be transformed by the renewing of your mind . . ." (Romans 12:2).

Only a daily, thorough examination can reverse the downward spiral. If we fall short of that, we must accept the consequence of running with the world: being condemned with it. "But when we are judged, we are disciplined by the Lord in order that we may not be condemned along with the world" (1 Corinthians 11:32).

The world is not quite as harmless as we'd like to think. Of the affluence that pervades the twentieth-century church, we could say with Ryle:

> [Is it] not true that nothing damages the cause of religion so much as "the world"? It is not open sin, or open unbelief, which robs Christ of his professing servants, so much as the love of the world, the fear of the world, the cares of the world, the business of the world, the money of the world, the pleasures of the world, and the desire to keep in with the world. This is the great rock on which thousands of young people are continually making shipwreck. They do not object to any article of the Christian faith. They do not deliberately choose evil and openly rebel against God. They hope somehow to get to heaven at last, and they think it proper to have some religion. But they cannot give up their idol: they must have the world. And so after running well and bidding fair for heaven while boys and girls, they turn aside when they become men and women and go down the broad way which leads to destruction.

Passivism. On the dusty road where Jesus pointed out that a would-be disciple could not follow him and delight in the world's goods, the Master turned to another and said, "Follow Me." Obviously this man had overheard the previous conversation and had already counted the cost. To him it looked like little more than an invitation to deprivation, so he responded: "Permit me first to go and bury my father." But Jesus said to him, "Allow the dead to bury their own dead; but as for you, go and proclaim everywhere the kingdom of God" (Luke 9:59, 60).

Before you think Jesus made an unreal demand on this

man, understand that his father was not yet dead. In that day, burial took place on the day of death. For practicality, as much as anything else, there was no embalming. The man was not really claiming his father had died. He really meant, Jesus, I would really like to come. But it's not convenient right now. My dad's a bit older. I think I ought to stay and take care of him first. When I no longer feel that responsibility—at a more convenient time—I will catch up with You. The man who wanted to wait had fallen into passivism—do-nothing-ism. He could have given any other reason that would not have mattered, but his response amounted to little more than straight-arming Jesus' call—because he didn't like His timing.

Sentimentalism. The third would-be follower tried to condition his commitment: "And another also said, 'I will follow You, Lord; but first permit me to say good-bye to those at home.' But Jesus said to him, 'No one, after putting his hand to the plow and looking back, is fit for the kingdom of God' " (Luke 9:61, 62).

Home, what a beautiful, sentimental word. The things there are precious . . . and dear . . . and good. But they may also become a major deterrent to discipleship, if we give them first place in our lives. Our fondness for family and wordly goods ought not to have such a hold on our lives that they pull us away from the One who loved us so much that He left a heavenly home to redeem us.

Though we want to enjoy family and do for family, too often that diminishes our commitment to Christ. In the press for things, we pay the price by cheating someone or something else. Sad to say, it's easiest to cheat God. So we put Him off. Charles Haddon Spurgeon reminds us of the terrible end of such sentimentalism:

> You are only young apprentices at present, and when your time is out you think it will be early enough to attend to matters of soul-interest. Or you are only journeymen at present, and when you have earned sufficient money to set you up in business then will be the time to think of God. Or you are little masters and have just begun business; you have a rising family and are struggling hard, and this is

your pretense for procrastination. You promise that when
you have a competence and can quietly retire to a snug
little villa in the country and your children have grown up,
then you will repent of the past and seek God's grace for
the future. All these are self-delusions of the grossest kind,
for you will do no such thing. What you are today you will
probably be tomorrow, and what you are tomorrow, you
will probably be the next day, and unless a miracle
happens—that is to say, unless the supernatural grace of
God shall make a new man of you—you will be at your last
day what you now are: without God, without hope, and a
stranger to the commonwealth of Israel. Procrastination is
the greatest of Satan's nets; in this he catcheth more un-
wary souls than in any other.

Anything we love more than Him will disappoint us in
the end and move us from our heavenly goal. The choice
is ours. . . .

The Prospect for Discipleship

He is Lord; the empty tomb leaves no room for doubt.
Lordship demands discipleship. While all of us fall short
of everything that entails, we cannot allow ourselves or
anyone else to think Jesus settles for anything less.

Whether or not we live as disciples has a great impact on
our lives. Look at two men who took different roads.

On a journey to Damascus, a vindictive rabbi named
Saul met the Living Christ, and his life would never be the
same. He took the disciple's path, and his writings attest
that he paid the price and encountered numerous perils
along the way.

Just weeks before his death, he penned a note to his
young friend and fellow disciple Timothy. Under the
shadow of the executioner's blade, Paul wrote: "I have
fought the good fight, I have finished the course. I have
kept the faith" (2 Timothy 4:7). His course, a hard a rigorous one . . . blood and tears every step of the way. No
flowery beds of ease for Paul . . . no easy way. Reflecting
on his walk with Christ, Paul remembered:

. . . Imprisonments, beaten times without number, often in danger of death. Five times I received from the Jews thirty-nine lashes. Three times I was beaten with rods, once I was stoned, three times I was shipwrecked, a night and a day I have spent in the deep. I have been on frequent journeys, in dangers from rivers, dangers from robbers, dangers from my countrymen, dangers from the Gentiles, dangers in the city, dangers in the wilderness, dangers on the sea, dangers among false brethren; I have been in labor and hardship, through many sleepless nights, in hunger and thirst, often without food, in cold and exposure.

2 Corinthians 11:23–27

At the end, looking back on it all, he wrote, "I have no regrets, Timothy. I have finished the course."

Paul had purposed to go the distance. As his end lay in sight, he knew what lay beyond: "In the future there is laid up for me the crown of righteousness, which the Lord, the righteous Judge, will award to me on that day . . ."(2 Timothy 4:8). He pictured coming to the end of the race . . . breaking the tape . . . and receiving the prize. Though he had not yet completed the course, that assurance drove him on. It enabled Paul to look beyond the temporal and lay hold of the eternal. For you and me, the course still unfolds . . . in the future lies a crown.

But not all who run finish the course.

Robby was only a child, when his father died. Because she lacked means to properly raise and educate her son, his mother sent him off to London to learn a trade; and the boy did well as a barber's apprentice.

Like most young men in a big city, Robby became caught up in the pursuits and pleasures of the world. But one evening, at a friend's invitation, Robby Robinson went to hear George Whitefield preach. At the end of the service, Robby responded to the gospel, claiming Christ as Lord and Savior. So sincere was he that he eventually returned to school and received a sound theological education.

By the time he was twenty-five years old, Robert Robin-son pastored the prestigious Baptist Church at Cambridge. During his successful and influential ministry, he penned some words still sung today:

> *Come, Thou Fount of ev'ry blessing,*
> *Tune my heart to sing Thy grace;*
> *Streams of mercy, never ceasing,*
> *Call for songs of loudest praise.*

Many years later, a wealthy woman, traveling by coach through England, felt particularly moved by the words of that hymn as she read them in a devotional book. Turning to a much older man who happened to be traveling in the same coach, she asked what he thought of the hymn.

With tears, he replied, "Madam, I am the poor, un-happy man who wrote that hymn years ago, and I'd give a thousand worlds, if I had them, to enjoy the feelings I had then."

Carnality and spiritual instability had spotted and stained Robinson's life and ministry. *Why?* we wonder. *Why such a fall for one who seemed so committed?*

Robinson supplied the answer himself . . . in the same song, which ends: "Prone to wander—Lord, I feel it—Prone to leave the God I love. . . ."

I, too, am so prone . . .

> *Lord Jesus,*
> *Grant me the grace of fidelity.*
> *Help me lengthen my stride*
> *In this walk with You.*

Nine

To the
Discipline!

More than twenty-five years ago, I was a young
novice at Saint Paul's Monastery in Pittsburgh, Pennsylvania. . . .

Only a few minutes past 2:00 A.M., our community bell
had roused all the monks—as it did every morning at that
hour—and summoned us to the monastery chapel. Once
assembled, we began chanting antiphonally, and in Latin,
the psalms, readings, and prayers prescribed for this first
hour of the divine office, Matins and Lauds.

On this particular morning, as we gave ourselves to the
somewhat longer and much more beautiful Gregorian
chant, a small group of retreatants entered the chapel.
These Catholic laymen had come apart to spend a weekend in silence and solitude, to examine their spiritual lives
and standing before God. For whatever reason—which
certainly would have made no sense to us younger monks,
who would surely have preferred sleeping to chanting—
these zealous men chose to interrupt their sleep to more
fully share the rigors of monastic life.

The novitiate marked my second major step in the journey to priesthood. At that time—pre-Vatican II—one cus-

tomarily became a novice in the Eastern Province of the Passionist Fathers after six years of postulancy at Holy Cross Seminary in Dunkirk, New York. No little excitement accompanied the vestiture ceremony, in which the postulant was clothed in the religious habit of the Passionists and received into the community as a novice—a beginner.

I can only compare those days at Saint Paul's to a sort of spiritual boot camp. Like the marines, the Passionists did not look for great numbers, just a few good men! Even as they received our class, we all knew not all twenty-four of us would reach the third step and profess vows as a Passionist.

In fact, our ranks were thinned simply but most effectively. It was all a matter of discipline. . . .

The Passionists had a deep appreciation for the spiritual warfare John alluded to: "Do not love the world, nor the things of the world. If anyone loves the world, the love of the Father is not in him. For all that is in the world, the lust of the flesh and the lust of the eyes and the boastful pride of life, is not from the Father, but is from the world" (1 John 2:15, 16). Our superiors understood that this troika of evil—the lust of the flesh, the lust of the eyes, and the boastful pride of life—posed a terrible threat to growth in the Christian life. Because of this the Passionists committed themselves to discipline as the chief means by which they might subdue the flesh and allow the Spirit of God to develop in them the image of Christ.

The framework for much of this discipline was the day-to-day routine of community religious life. A typical day—and most of them were *very* typical—looked like this:

5:45 A.M.	Rise—call to chapel
6:00	Chanting Prime/the sung Martyrology
6:30	First Mass—Mass of communion
7:00	Second Mass—Mass of thanksgiving
7:30	Breakfast—standing and in silence
7:45	Return to cell—prepare for the day
8:00	Classes—academic and/or spiritual
11:30	Chanting Tierce, Sext, None

12:00	Noon meal—in silence
12:30 P.M.	Thanksgiving prayers in chapel
12:40	Community recreation—most often two by two
1:15	Vesper rest
2:15	Rise—call to chapel
2:30	Chanting Vespers/brief meditation
3:00	Rosary procession in monastery gardens
3:15	Study and/or quiet time
5:15	Solitary walk
5:30	Chanting Compline/meditation
6:00	Evening meal—in silence
6:30	Thanksgiving prayers in chapel
6:40	Community recreation—most often two by two
7:15	Study and/or quiet time
9:00	Nightly benediction
9:10	Retire to cell for the evening
2:00 A.M.	Rise—call to chapel
2:15	Chanting Matins and Lauds/meditation
3:00	Return to cell until Prime

While this schedule most accurately depicts a day in the novitiate, with very few changes, it also depicts the routine of most Passionist monasteries, prior to Vatican II, which relaxed many monastic rules and observances.

On the day the retreatants visited us, at the conclusion of Matins and Lauds,we sat down to spend the rest of the hour in silent prayer and meditation. When the small chapel clock chimed three, the Father Rector, to signal our dismissal, knocked on the lectern before him and said in Latin: *"Ad disciplinam!"* Though only a prepositional phrase, those two words carried the weight of an imperative, "To the discipline!" In his own way, Father Martin Joseph humorously reminded us that while our guests could now retire to their rooms, we still had one more monastic practice to observe before we could return to bed—*the discipline.*

Those words referred to one specific ascetic exercise, which Passionists saw as part of the warfare against the

lust of the flesh. Twice Paul alludes to a physical discipline: "But I buffet my body and make it my slave . . ." (1
Corinthians 9:27); "Now those who belong to Christ Jesus
have crucified the flesh with its passions and desires"
(Galatians 5:24).

When the Father Rector sent us to the discipline, he
instructed each monk to return to his cell and apply the
flagellum—a small, whiplike instrument with five stingers, each approximately the size of a man's little finger and
woven of several strands of tight white cord. Each stinger
was suspended from an eight-inch lead cord, which joined
the others at the base of a four-inch braided handle. The
discipline was held in the right hand and applied by vig-
orously moving the hand from side to side and allowing
the stingers to fall on one's bare back. It was administered
three times a week (Monday, Wednesday, and Friday) . . .
immediately following Matins and Lauds . . . in the pri-
vacy of one's own cell . . . and for the duration of five
paters (Our Fathers), five *aves* (Hail Marys), and the *Mise-
rere* (Psalm 51).

I do not wish to justify or condemn the scourge. But as
a group, we recognized that a war truly waged within our
own members. With the discipline, we expressed our desire to have the lusts of the flesh subject to our wills as we
sought to yield them to His.

We also realized that most of us want what we see . . .
ownership notwithstanding . . . the "lust of the eyes."
Because we understood that the eye gate could feed a
concupiscent heart, we committed ourselves to limiting
access through that gate. To help us gain mastery over
those two wanderers, as novices we were not allowed to
look one another in the eyes, an ascetic practice known as
"mortification of the eyes." We had to learn to hold our
heads high, but cast our eyes downward, so that we would
not see faces or lock eyes. This practice not only sought to
safeguard our minds and hearts, from external and hostile
influences, but also helped prepare us for a life-style that
chose to say no to self.

We learned early on in monastic life that John's "boastful

pride of life" is the religion of all who enshrine self as lord. The schedule, flagellum, mortification of the eyes, along with silence, tiny cells with straw-filled mattresses as beds, solitude, and vows of poverty, chastity, and obedience were all, in the final analysis, aimed at restraining pride.

On the day we professed our vows, the Novice Master placed a cross on our shoulders as Father Rector charged us: "Receive dearest Brother, the Cross of Our Lord Jesus Christ: deny yourself. . . ." As the crown of thorns was placed on our heads, he continued: "Accept dearest Brother, the crown of thorns of Christ our Lord. Humble yourself under the powerful hand of God, and be subject to every creature for the love of God. Amen." Whether we agree with nothing else, two phrases in these exhortations are certainly key to the disciplined life—*"deny yourself . . ." "humble yourself. . . ."*

A Call to the Disciplined Life

Well, that was all more than a quarter of a century ago. The scourge, straw-filled mattresses, silence, solitude—even the celibacy—are all behind me. But the effects of those disciplined years linger. Much older now and I hope a bit wiser, I know how sorely I needed discipline during those formative years . . . and how much *more* I need it now!

Discipline conjures up many and varied images. To a child it might suggest a lengthy list of *do's* and *don'ts* . . . to parents, their ongoing struggle with a firm kindness and a kind firmness . . . to an athlete, the agony of steeling himself for the contest . . . to a drill sergeant, the rigorous training necessary to transform raw recruits into ready marines . . . to the professor, a science or body of knowledge to be mastered . . . and to church leaders it might recall the scriptural mandate to protect the purity and integrity of the visible church.

Webster's dictionary clearly endorses all these ideas in its definition: "instruction . . . a subject that is taught . . . training that corrects, molds, or perfects the mental faculties or moral character . . . punishment . . . a rule or system of rules governing conduct . . . self-control." Yet as Christians we even need to go beyond these. Discipline ought to speak of our carriage before a watching world as well as our commitment to a loving Lord.

To be painfully honest, not only does the church need to recover worship but even a cursory study of the twentieth-century church reveals that any sense of prolonged and purposeful discipline has all but vanished!

In the late fifties and early sixties, Augustine Paul Hennessy—a theologian unknown to most evangelicals—began to speak of a *mollitia*, a softness, that he saw overtaking the church. Well, it's here . . . we have been overtaken. We hear precious little about discipline . . . and see even less.

Please do not misunderstand: I am not advocating celibacy, straw sacks, and self-flagellation. But I am convinced today's evangelical church exhibits a terrible lack of discipline.

The church *needs* discipline—mentally . . . physically . . . and spiritually. The apostle once known as Simon, later renamed Peter, the Rock, by the Master, challenges us to it.

Mental Discipline

Peter described mental discipline when he penned the words: "Therefore gird your minds for action, keep sober in spirit . . ." (1 Peter 1:13).

Know that he wrote in a time when men wore long, flowing robes. If they wanted to quicken their pace or become involved in strenuous activity, they had to lift their robes and tighten them—gird them—at their waists. Only then could they move about freely.

To move in and about our high-speed and sophisticated society our minds, too, must be girded for the task.

Paul Little, a great man of God and contender for the faith, wrote two books that did battle with intellectuals on their own territory; they were called *Know What You Believe* and *Know Why You Believe*. I believe today's church has not taken the challenge of those volumes seriously enough. Too many cannot clearly and concisely articulate what they believe; even fewer can explain *why*.

I fear that we—the church—must take responsibility for this, because in reacting to main-line denominationalism and its formalities, we have substituted cute phrases and canned formulas for serious and systematic study of ". . . the faith which was once for all delivered to the saints" (Jude 3). In rebelling against the catechism, we have also relegated catechesis to the realm of the unimportant. Have we made certain the faith delivered to and preserved by the saints of an earlier day is truly passed on, examined, and treasured by the saints of today? Are we involved in firsthand study on a daily basis . . . or do we merely ingest predigested truths each Sunday? Have we trained our children in biblical truth and living . . . or do we confuse them with our own enculturated Christianity of traditions and laws? Only those who gird their minds will even ask such questions!

". . . Gird your minds for action, keep sober in spirit. . . ." The phrase "in spirit" does not actually appear in the original; the text simply reads "stay sober." While the Greek verb certainly includes the idea of keeping oneself free from the effects of intoxicating beverages, even more basic to the word is the idea of being self-controlled and well balanced. Not only should we avoid liquor, but no intoxicating or deluding thoughts should allow us to escape reality and evade the call of Christ in every area of our lives.

The apostle means, "Equip yourselves mentally for the battlefield around you and maintain a balanced world view. Keep the essential steadiness, the stability of mind that characterizes the person who knows what he or she believes . . . and lives by it." Without that balance, we will become the double-minded people of whom James wrote. Only a world view with God at the center keeps us from being unstable in all our ways.

Too many of us become double minded. Effective witnesses for Christ need stable minds . . . convictions. The world still stands up and takes notice of the man or woman who says: "These are my convictions. On these I stand, I can do no other."

The mental discipline Peter writes about is the pursuit of God. If we wish to achieve it in our lives, we will seek to increase our knowledge of Him, making Him our greatest focus in life. Charles Haddon Spurgeon described the person with this outlook:

> He who thinks often of God will have a larger mind than the man who simply plods around this narrow globe. . . . The most excellent study for expanding the soul is the science of Christ, and Him crucified, and the knowledge of the Godhead in the glorious Trinity. Nothing will so enlarge the intellect, nothing so magnify the whole soul of man, as a devout, earnest, continued investigation of the great subject of the Deity.

What a challenge! But with the knowledge of God comes an ever-present companion—the task of articulating our faith to those around us. To do that we must prepare to meet others on their own territory—in their own interest fields. He will be our *great* focus, but not our only one; we need education in the arts and sciences, too.

C. S. Lewis reminds us:

> If all the world were Christian it might not matter if all the world were uneducated. But, as it is, a cultural life will exist outside the church whether it exists inside or not. To be ignorant and simple now—not to be able to meet the enemies on their own ground—would be to throw down our weapons, and to betray our uneducated brethren who have, under God, no defense but us against the intellectual attacks of the heathen.

When we meet people who don't speak our language, we must be prepared to speak theirs.

Recently a friend sent me an article titled: "Sixty Novels for Your Shelves," which listed books selected by the editorial board of the Book-of-the-Month Club because they "not only defined an American character, but shaped the way a generation acts and talks." My friend's note read: "John—How many have you read?" To my shame, six!

How many of us read quality contemporary literature . . . take advantage of the many cultural opportunities afforded us by the fine museums in our great cities . . . familiarize ourselves with great masterpieces of art and music? My own ministry has, at times, been limited by my lack of exposure to the arts.

We cannot take this lightly. The arts and sciences are indeed fertile ground for sharing our faith in a personal and powerful God, whose Son died on the cross, then rose from the dead. That faith did not require that we vacate our minds and withdraw from the world. Far from it! Disciplining our minds begins by recognizing that all truth is God's truth, then determining to articulate faith intelligently in an unbelieving world. C. S. Lewis was right—for a Christian, the learned and informed life is an obligation!

Physical Discipline

"As obedient children, do not be conformed to the former lusts . . . ," the apostle continues (1 Peter 1:14).

In Romans, Paul urged us not to be conformed to this world—not to get squeezed into its mold . . . boxed in by its scheme of things. Using the same Greek verb, Peter now warns us not to let our lusts box us in, either.

When it comes to physical discipline, we can cut no slack. The military trained me to engage the enemy at the forward edge of battle area and I need the same outlook on my faith. Because I am a Christian I am ever exposed to the attacks of the enemy and cannot become lax. Every day I face subtle temptations . . . and a swift fall.

Avoiding the Lust of the Eyes

Of the lust of the flesh, lust of the eyes, and the boastful pride of life, the enemy's principle technique remains the lust of the eyes. How much of our difficulty begins with the eyes! In this gateway to the soul, desires kindle and are fueled until our wills can no longer resist their intensity. The pattern is ever the same. Let's look briefly at three familiar examples. First, Eve: "When the woman saw that the tree was good for food, and that it was a delight to the eyes, and that the tree was desirable to make one wise, she took from its fruit and ate . . ." (Genesis 3:6). Then Achan, in his own words: "When I saw among the spoil a beautiful mantle from Shinar and two hundred shekels of silver and a bar of gold fifty shekels in weight, then I coveted them and took them . . ." (Joshua 7:21). Finally, King David: "Now when evening came David arose from his bed and walked around on the roof of the king's house, and from the roof he saw a woman bathing; and the woman was very beautiful in appearance. So David sent and inquired about the woman. And one said, 'Is this not Bathsheba, the daughter of Eliam, the wife of Uriah the Hittite?' And David sent messengers and took her . . ." (2 Samuel 11:2–4).

We need only examine the key words and phrases in each narrative to see that the steps are essentially the same: sight, attraction or overdesire, and surrender.

Eve—she saw . . . a delight/desirable . . . she took
Achan—I saw . . . I coveted . . . I took
David—he saw . . . very beautiful in appearance . . . he
took

In each situation lustful eyes fed both the lust of the flesh and boastful pride. For Eve, the forbidden tree was good for food (*flesh*) and capable of imparting wisdom (*pride*). Achan took goods under the ban for the life of leisure (*flesh*) and prestige (*pride*) they might afford. David, as king, set himself above the law (*pride*) and slept with Uriah's wife (*flesh*).

Job understood the threat the eye gate posed. For him it was a matter of personal determination and discipline: "I have made a covenant with my eyes . . ." (Job 31:1). We must do the same. A short walk through any busy mall or on any city street amounts to little more than sensory overload. Unless we are highly disciplined, with every step we receive signals—not always subtle—that appeal to either our flesh or our pride. If we open ourselves to these suggestions, we *will* yield—or be slowly conditioned to yield— in thought or deed before we even become aware we have done so. Only such a covenant can keep us from harm.

Maximum-Health Discipline

Certainly keeping the body pure is another important part of physical discipline. As Christians we should not simply discard that as "unspiritual" and avoid caring for these "temples of the living God." What we put into our bodies and how they look can make powerful testimonies to a watching world.

Within evangelical circles we find it far too easy to let this slide. The Protestant work ethic makes it difficult at times to *play* . . . involvement with family and time spent at church make it rather easy to rule out *exercise* . . . and personal desires to achieve, to work harder, and reach higher eliminate any hope of or time for *rest* . . . because our gatherings almost always include food, *diet* also becomes just about impossible.

Too many of us take physical health for granted. For most of us, the absence of disease or *dis-ease,* the lack of symptoms, complaints, illness, or discomfort means we are healthy. While that may mean health, it is only minimum health.

Not only should we make the absence of illness our goal, we should strive for maximum health for an optimal quality of life. Unfortunately, most of us do not feel sufficiently motivated to care for our bodies as we ought, until a tragedy such as a heart attack or some preventable medical condition afflicts us or some significant other in our lives.

Worse still, for too long Christians have been more concerned with whether one uses tobacco or alcohol than with weight and appearance. Rarely, if ever have we seen them as spiritual problems indicative of self-indulgence and indolence, but in most cases that is exactly what they are. We have also chosen to applaud and uphold as models, the hard-charging drivers—especially those in ministry—despite the fact that in their zeal they, too, abuse their bodies.

Beginning to say yes to beneficial things—and no to harmful things is never easy. Each of us knows whether we push our bodies or pamper them, and either extreme might well indicate a lack of discipline. Let me simply suggest that you consider the four words I mentioned already: *exercise, diet, rest,* and *play.*

Exercise. On my desk sits an oblong paperweight that reads: "It's fun to run." No it is *not* fun to run. I hate it—it's one of the most painful experiences of my life . . . second only to visiting an oral surgeon. Yet when we think exercise, most of us think of running. Not everyone can run . . . and not everyone should run. Certainly no one who has been sedentary for a long period of time should begin a strenuous program of exercise. . . .

But unless we have a medical order not to, all of us can begin a modified program of exercise. For some it might be calisthenics . . . for others walking . . . some might prefer swimming . . . or whatever. But we all ought to try to keep ourselves in shape. When Paul wrote, "For bodily discipline is only of little profit, but godliness is profitable for all things . . ." (1 Timothy 4:8), he did not disparage physical exercise. Rather, he stressed that the discipline of godliness had even greater value. The truth is the inspired text teaches that physical exercise *does* profit the body!

Diet. Nobody dislikes diets more than I. As I pen these words it is Thanksgiving Eve—in a sense the entrance to almost five weeks of holidays, with all gatherings, special meals, and treats. And I am on a diet! My family feels convinced I'll be on one for the rest of my life. But diets, too, have their place. I once saw a poster that read: "Diets are for people who are thick . . . and tired of it!"

In his letter to the church at Rome, Paul made it very clear there was more to the kingdom of God than our liberty in eating and drinking. As a matter of fact, in the Sermon on the Mount, the Master Himself said: "Do not be anxious for your life, as to what you shall eat, or what you shall drink . . . Is not life more than food . . . ? (Matthew 6:25). It really is! Once we begin to curb our appetites, we will be amazed how much better we feel about ourselves.

Haddon Robinson, well-known churchman and speaker, has a daughter who once had a weight problem, but is now beautifully trim and employed as a professional model. When he asked her how she managed to keep the weight off, she replied: "No food ever tasted as good as being thin feels!"

After I completed my last diet—the one just before this one—my children gave me a card that congratulated me for just winning *The No-Belly Prize*. This time around I'm committed to balance—to be careful about what I eat—and when—and how much. I'm learning that this discipline is, in fact, a genuine spiritual concern.

Rest. Life in the fast lane will get you. There is simply too much stress—and stress kills. In a quiet moment, after a busy day, Jesus gathered His men and said: "Come apart to a lovely place and rest awhile" (*see* Mark 6:31). Commenting on this verse, Vance Havner said: "Jesus was really saying: 'Come apart . . . before you come apart!' "

Quite possibly this is what the writer intended when he wrote: "Slow me down, Lord, and inspire me to send my roots deep into the soil of life's enduring values that I may grow toward my greater destiny. Remind me each day that the race is not always to the swift . . . and that there is more to life than increasing its speed!"

Play. Somehow we have grown up thinking of this as a pastime only for children—but it's not. There is something so therapeutic—so healthy for the whole man—in laughter and play. Maybe that is why Solomon, reflecting on the futility and fleeting nature of life, said: "There is an appointed time for everything. . . . A time to laugh . . . and a time to dance" (Ecclesiastes 3:1, 4). I heartily recommend it.

I agree with that monk, Friar Anonymous, who wrote:

> If I had my life to live over again . . . I would be sillier than I've been this trip.

I know of very few things I would take seriously . . .
I would climb more mountains, swim more rivers, and
watch more sunsets. I would do more walking and
looking. . . . If I had my life to live over, I would start
barefoot in the spring and stay that way later in the fall. I
would play hooky more . . . I would ride on more mer-
ry-go-rounds . . . I would pick more daisies.

Obviously this man had his fill of stress. What a telling
phrase: "If I had my life to live over. . . ." We don't . . .
none of us! But those words invite you to quit the rat race.

Spiritual Discipline

While both mental and physical discipline are genuine
spiritual concerns, Peter ends by challenging us with our
chief spiritual discipline: "But like the Holy One who
called you, be holy yourselves also in all your behavior;
because it is written, 'You shall be holy, for I am holy' " (1
Peter 1:15, 16).

Because it is of the very essence and nature of God and
only He can give it, God invites each of us to share in His
holiness. We cannot earn it, or by human effort make
ourselves holy. But we can place ourselves in an arena in
which He can impart holiness. Spiritual discipline alone
enables us to consistently present ourselves to Him so that
He might continue the process of sanctification in our
lives. From the beginning, He has intended to imprint on
us the character of His own dear Son. His chief desire
manward is that we become a distinctive people . . . a
holy people . . . His people. But, this does not just happen.

Although growth in holiness is completely grace—
uniquely and solely the work of God in the life of His
children—we must commit ourselves to meeting Him in
the arenas He has chosen: prayer and meditation . . . the
reading and study of His holy Word . . . individual and
corporate worship . . . silence and solitude . . . and service and fellowship.

None of this comes naturally or easily. If it did, we
would have no need for grace . . . no need for discipline.

Drawing near to God and allowing Him to reproduce His own life in us requires of us a discipline of the highest order—but even that discipline will require first from Him the grace of fidelity.

Early in my pastoral ministry, God used Rose to teach me a most important lesson. As we were driving down Golf Course Hill in Windsor, Vermont, both of us more than just a bit weary and worn from the work of the ministry, Rose asked softly: "Have you noticed how we've become so busy in the ministry that we spend little time with the Master?"

Fifteen years later that still remains one of the greatest challenges of my pastoral ministry—making time to be alone with the Master. Of all my relationships this one is certainly the most difficult to maintain—because I can most easily put it off. Because it is strictly between God and me, too often I allow that area to slide first.

On more Sundays that I care to admit, my dryness primarily results from my own neglect of the spiritual disciplines. At the end of one such week, overwhelmed with a sense that my well had truly dried up, I penned this psalm:

> In my mind's eye, Lord
> I see the faces of your children
> assembling this Lord's Day
> to worship You,
> to experience Your Presence
> as they encounter You in Your Word.

> Some will come excited
> expecting to meet You.
> Many will join us straight from battle—
> *contra mundum*—
> bruised and battered from that conflict.
> Others will be here out of sheer routine,
> anticipation at a real low.
> Still others driven here by an inner longing
> only You can fill.

Lord God, I do not, and will not, exaggerate my
role.
No good can be accomplished,
no ministry effected
apart from You.
Nonetheless, that small part You've entrusted to
me
deserves my best.
And now, as Sunday draws near,
I hear the awful accusations of
a text not fully grasped,
an outline still incomplete,
a title not selected,
words as yet unpenned.
The wells are dry.

Reasons surface—quickly . . .
A swift-paced summer
that didn't deliver the relaxed schedule
it seemed to promise at first;
a pile of paperwork
that kept me from Your Word;
the beauty of these glorious days
that seduce the mind
and somehow drain its creative energies;
the desire, and need, to put my mind in neutral
after the mental, emotional,
and spiritual activity of a long day.

But Lord, You are making it quite clear
these reasons are mine.
It is my voice I've heard,
not that of my Advocate.
I have succumbed
to a loyalty to lesser loves.
I agree with You, Father.
I have chosen the good over the Best.

These dry wells are of my own doing.
I am without excuse.

Many of us in pastoral ministry know full well the pain
of coming before God's people and trying to speak a word

from Him when we have not first spoken *with Him.* Simply, we cannot give what we do not have . . . and we cannot lead a people anywhere we have not gone ourselves. Periodically, regularly I have to renew my resolve to spend the first half hour of each day in prayer . . . and that is not enough.

I have been challenged greatly by the example of my good friend and brother in the ministry, David Fisher. This busy pastor of a large and growing church has a highly structured hour and a half that he devotes each day to spiritual exercises.

David begins with readings from the Psalter and several selections from the *Diary of Private Prayers,* by John Baillie. Then he turns to his personal prayer book, where he reads not only from his own reflections and meditations, but also from a collection of the great prayers of the church— the *Te Deum,* the *Veni Creator,* and the *Gloria in Excelsis.* These serve as his introit into the presence of God. After personal communion with God comes a period of intercession. David concludes with a brief study in two areas— the first systematic theology and the second either biblical studies or a biography of one of the saints.

Unfortunately, too many of us become spiritual Marthas, not Marys. Like Martha, we forget that though we need to do those important ministries and care for the Guest, knowing when to stop and spend time with the Savior is also a part of a proper spiritual balance. Mary, sitting at the feet of Jesus, had a better outlook on the Master. Like her, my greatest need is to position myself at His feet, so He can equip and grow me for His purposes.

During a time of great pressure in my life, the wife of a close friend wrote what seemed to be a prophetic word for me:

> *Merry-go-round of ministry,*
> *Will you ever stop?*
> *It seems there is an eternal line*
> *Of those who need a ride.*

The crowds and throngs of people
Are ever pressing near.
Will there ever be a stop
To this twirling human motion?

Yes, My child, if you will only
Come apart awhile with Me,
You will hear My voice above all others,
I will care for all these needs.

I want you to step off this
Merry-go-round of ministry.
It is not My will for you
To spin and twirl through life.

My child, walk as I did upon earth
Take time to come apart,
To listen, to be with those you love,
I have other servants to do the work.

Come away with Me, My child.
Walk in the stillness of My Presence.
For I have instructed you: In quietness
And confidence shall be your strength.

When we become too busy to spend time with Jesus, we
are just plain *too busy.* As we thrust away prayer, Bible
study, and other disciplines, in search of time for ministry,
we lose our strength in Christ and no longer experience an
incessant longing for Him.

In an impressive list of men and women who have known
the disciplined life, Hebrews 11 speaks of those who by
faith exercised their minds for His glory . . . endured great
suffering for His name . . . and evidenced a longing for
His Person that enabled them to choose death that they
might live with Him. According to that text, the world was
not worthy of these great heroes, who gained His approval.
Later the writer tells us why they suffered: "All discipline
for the moment seems not to be joyful, but sorrowful; yet
to those who have been trained by it, afterwards it yields
the peaceful fruit of righteousness" (Hebrews 12:11).

Ten

Walk On!

*I*t was a *Dear John* letter. But most of my letters come that way. . . .

Right next to the greeting, in bold letters, were the words: *for your eyes only*. That very familiar phrase harkened back to my days as an intelligence agent. I knew the letter was meant only for me. As I read on, I learned why—its author was going to point out a character flaw in my life . . . , and he was kind and gracious enough to want to do that privately. Knowing he would not object, I would like to share some of that letter with you.

Looking back after breakfast, I found myself unhappy— I am sure you probably felt the same. . . .

I feel you have much on your side. I have seen you walk the extra mile. . . .

John, please remember that not everyone acts as you do. Your *actions* to me are generally very praiseworthy, but, at times, your *reactions* leave much to be desired. If outside factors interfere with what we would like—it just goes with the territory. I know it is hard to understand the actions of others, but I do not think we should allow that to interrupt relationships.

Normally, that kind of observation is neither easy to take or to lay out before others. But the author had the *right* to say those things—and he did so gently. I placed a great deal of stock in his comments. He concluded:

> I love you very much. I don't want to ever see you so upset again. Love, hugs, 'n xxxx's, Dad.

The breakfast Dad referred to had been painful. He sensed I had become more than just a little upset with my sister about something I regarded as terribly inconsiderate and unthinking on her part. In his soft and quiet way, Dad told me how deeply pained he was to know that two of his children were upset with each other. While he readily understood why I felt hurt, he could not excuse the fact that I had noticeably withdrawn from my sister—my calls to her were fewer . . . and our July outing to her part of the country even skirted her little town.

He was right. I knew it even as I read his letter. But the wound still went deep. I could so easily justify my silence. So I folded the letter, tucked it back in its envelope, and placed it in my desk drawer, along with other precious notes from Mom and Dad.

Nine months later, going through my desk, I found and reread his letter. By then it had become even more apparent Dad had been right from the very beginning. I quickly took a piece of stationery and wrote to my sister:

> *Little things are not important. . . .*
> *Big sisters are!*
> *I really love you.*

Even as I penned those words, I found it difficult to believe I had allowed such an insignificant slight to come between my sister and myself. Almost immediately I called to let her know a note was on its way. She sounded so very happy that I had taken time to call, but she still had no idea as to why I had been upset. I simply told her it was a matter so small I would feel ashamed to tell her. With that, nine wasted months came to an end.

Then I called Dad. Even though it had taken me so long

to follow through on his words of wisdom, he was delighted to know we had healed a painful separation. The very special joy in his voice made me realize how deeply my carnality and immaturity had hurt him. That day I learned a little more about the biblical precept of honoring one's father.

Just about three months later, one Tuesday evening, I called Mom and Dad at their summer home in Vermont. When Mom answered the phone, she mentioned Dad had said only Sunday that he wanted to talk to his boys. As soon as he came to the phone, I told him I thought it was time for the whole family to enjoy a conference call. By simply punching several numbers on my hand phone, Dad and I were soon linked up with brother, Alan. With a few more numbers, sister Irene was with us as well. We will long remember that call. . . .

Dad was really at his best. His memory went back ten, twenty, thirty, and forty years. We laughed, recalling some of the crazy things we children had put him and Mom through. We marveled, as ever, about how different the three of us were. *Surely,* each one of us thought, *one of the other two must have been adopted.* Despite the distance, the miracle of telecommunications brought us very close together. Even more the warmth and love told Dad how really close his children were. I know the closing of that conversation must have been especially dear to Dad as he heard each of his children say to the other, and then to him, "I love you. . . ." What a special call. What a great deposit in our memory banks. We would need to draw on it soon. . . .

Thirty-six hours later, at about 2:00 A.M., the telephone interrupted my sleep. That is not unusual in the life of any of the Aker children—one a pastor, two involved in medical work. But the voice on the other end was Mom. I will never forget the pain in her voice: "John, I think Dad's gone."

Later that day, Irene, Alan, and I gathered together with Mom. Dad *was* gone—home with the Lord whom he loved so dearly and served so faithfully. I cannot help but think that, had it not been for Dad's letter encouraging me to get right with Irene, our meeting on that day would have been so much more difficult.

Since his death, Irene and I have several times discussed Dad's healing our relationship. As best we can both remember, that particular incident was the first true rift we had experienced in more than forty years as brother and sister. Don't get me wrong. Like most siblings, we have had our share of misunderstandings and quarrels—but rarely more than that. The truth of it is, Dad was too easily hurt by even the thought of his children not getting along with one another.

Alan never really had much of a struggle with that. He is quite tender, and a basic goodness and gentleness seem to keep him from getting embroiled in the *craziness*—as he would call it—of any kind of arguing. Irene and I, unfortunately, are wired somewhat differently. What seems to come rather naturally for Alan requires a more determined act of the will for us. But realizing how much pain our friction caused Dad, regardless of the issues, we have committed ourselves to maintaining loving and caring relationships. He would want it that way, simply because we are his children. In fact, we see this as one of the finest ways in which we can honor our father. . . .

In a very real way, all this carries over into my thinking on the church: I feel deeply about the fragmentation and fighting that takes place within Christendom. More, I believe we fail to recognize that we truly have, in the way we handle our differences and disagreements, a tremendous opportunity to honor our heavenly Father.

It was not easy for me to leave the Catholic Church. How *could* it have been? From the time I was a child at Saint Joseph's School, I was taught about Holy Mother, the church. Second only to that was the high regard we held for our earthly leader, the Holy Father. Both of those words—*mother* and *father*—are emotionally laden. Don't make the mistake of talking against my earthly mother or father; I would not respond well. Likewise, I seemed somewhat self-consciously programmed to not wanting to respond well to anyone who would speak ill of Holy Mother the Church or the Holy Father.

So God in His wisdom brought into our lives, through Mom and Dad, a couple who wanted to speak to us about *Jesus.* I was ready and willing to speak about, and listen to someone talk about *Jesus.* Had they even begun to speak about the church or the Pope, my guard would have gone up—and they probably would have gotten nowhere!

Even after my conversion experience, I returned to the Catholic Church. It was unthinkable that I would do otherwise. . . .

Weeks later, hungering for a greater exposure to the teaching of the Word of God, I timidly led my family to the New Village Congregational Church. As I approached a Protestant church for the first time, I did so half-expecting the roof to cleave and a lightning bolt from heaven to drop me in my tracks. As you can tell, that never happened. I received the spiritual nourishment and challenge I sensed I needed. Because of that, we continued to attend that church.

The struggles were not over. I missed a quiet and reverent atmosphere of worship . . . I longed for the mystery that accompanied so much of the liturgy . . . and I ached within at the thought of not being able to approach the altar rail and receive communion as I had done for years and years as a young Catholic.

But the people who led us to Christ were also faithful in answering some of those burning questions. Through them I came to a new understanding of the Lord's Supper. To me it still remains far more sacred than many seem to appreciate, but my comfort zone within evangelicalism grew.

Before long, I found myself being sought out to speak at church groups. There seemed to be a great deal of interest in this young man who had spent almost nine years in the monastery . . . served as an intelligence agent . . . and then came to know Christ. Why, people actually invited me to speak in their Sunday service and give my *testimony,* when I didn't even know what a *testimony* was!

Prompted by some friends and recognizing it afforded

me an opportunity to speak of my newfound relationship
with Jesus Christ, I accepted many of these invitations.
But, I found myself face to face with people who had
heard stories of Catholicism that were so very foreign to
me. As a young man, I had heard of Maria Monk and her
work, *Over the Wall*. But I now found myself meeting
people who actually believed those stories! One of my
friends presented me with James Beary's book, *The Monk
Who Lived Twice*.

Beary's work, like that of Mary Monk, was filled with
stories of clandestine meetings between monks and nuns
. . . political intrigue with the Vatican . . . and his own
efforts to elude the FBI and CIA, who were trying to keep
him under constant surveillance after his leaving the monastery. I could not believe what I was reading!

The FBI and CIA are not at all interested in the fact that
John Brian Aker, known in religious life as Confrater
André of Our Lady of the Holy Cross, left the Passionist
Fathers . . . nor are the Passionists monitoring my every
move to determine what I say about those days within the
monastery walls.

More than that I continue to bear affection for these dear
men with whom I spent those formative years of my life.
While I might now agree that I never heard a clear explanation of the gospel, I can honestly say that godly men
surrounded me—the young and old alike, who loved God
as they understood Him and were trying, through a life of
self-sacrifice, to please Him and atone for the sins of a
wicked world.

But the old hate stories have not ended—and wherever
a group chooses to feed on the debasing and the divisive,
the sensational and the secretive, there will always be a
storyteller on hand to satisfy their appetites.

I do not use the word *storyteller* lightly. Certainly a man
who chooses to speak of his past experiences ought to be
able to document them. The personal assertion that one
was once a monk, priest, or a bishop does not necessarily
make it so. In support of my claim that I was a Passionist,
I possess a document signed by Father Malcolm LaVelle,

Father General of the Passionist Congregation, in which he testifies that Confrater André of Our Lady of the Holy Cross, known in the world as John Brian Aker, was being released from his vows and allowed to return to secular life. To me it is a very important document. Even as I pen these words, I look at a copy before me on my desk.

Yet some who boast a similar background—or one of even greater stature within the Catholic Church—cannot produce verifiable evidence that they were, in fact, who they claimed to have once been.

Even a casual reading of their materials makes it quite clear that their stories are filled with inaccuracies, contradictions, and caricatures. Far from hearing about Christ's love that can save, heal, and make whole, I read instead the ravings of one filled with a hate that can only destroy and defile.

The most insidious form this has taken of late is a series of comic books (strange name—funny they are not) that tell a most bizarre tale. Those of you familiar with such materials must understand that we are teaching our children to hate—because these books, and other pamphlets like them, are filled with that kind of venom.

Please do not misunderstand me. I am not claiming orthodoxy and orthopraxy as the chief marks of the Catholic Church. I recognize the many discrepancies and ills within Catholicism. But what I feel more concerned about are the prejudices and presuppositions within evangelicals that make it difficult for us to communicate with non-evangelicals—especially Roman Catholics. Before we can ever engage in meaningful dialogue, we must prepare our hearts to love and our minds to seek truth.

The prejudices *are* there. . . .

As a young boy at Holy Cross Seminary, I remember being taught: *"Extra ecclesiam nulla salus"*—outside the church there is no salvation!" In short, unless you were Roman Catholic, you could *never* get to heaven. Now, I understood even the Catholics would have a tough road. Some, because of lives of devotion and good deeds, might find ready entrance into heaven. Others, because of godless lives filled with wickedness, would be banished to hell. I *knew* I would probably not make heaven on my first attempt. But I did not want to go to hell. I prayed for purgatory!

I felt so bad at times for my hell-bound next-door neighbors. Although, at times I certainly envied the fact that there seemed to be no sin in their religion—it did not really matter if they went to church every Sunday . . . or said certain prayers. I always had to be in church—not just on Sundays . . . but on the holy days of obligation as well! Yet in my own young mind, I just *knew* only Catholics would go to heaven anyway.

As I grew, my understanding of God's love broadened. It seemed quite apparent to me that a loving God would not—could not—send countless millions to hell *just* because they were not Catholic. *Surely,* I concluded, *those who honor God as they knew Him, and tried to do good to all men, would be acceptable to Him.* I felt comfortable with that—I did not need to bother proselytizing . . . or to pity those who had not had the fortune of being raised in or converted to Catholicism.

Within the monastery itself, I ascribed fully to Catholic doctrine. I saw the monastic life itself as man's attempt to earn salvation and somehow, through empathetic repentance, do penance for the sins of the entire world.

Then my conversion experience—for the first time I truly understood the uniqueness of Jesus. I saw in the sacred text where He Himself said: "Truly, truly, I say to you, unless one is born again, he cannot see the kingdom of God" (John 3:3). I always thought Billy Graham said that! Learning that the *Master* said unless I was *born again,* I could never enter the Kingdom of God, overwhelmed me.

As I continued my study of the fourth gospel, I read Jesus' words "I am the way, and the truth, and the life; no one comes to the Father but through Me" (14:6). With that came a deep and settled conviction that if a person had any other way to enter the kingdom of God, except through the completed work of Jesus Christ, His death on the cross became unnecessary. In other words, if even one person could gain access to heaven apart from that cross, any and all might do the same. If that were true, God—from my perspective—would be a murderer and a fool to allow His Son to undergo such a degrading unnecessary death.

Further examination of the Word of God—through Bible studies . . . retreats . . . seminars . . . worship at Bible-preaching churches—further *serious* study taught me more and more about this loving God. I began to understand that by grace alone a person could be saved. But—here some evangelicals may have difficulty with me—I believe that grace and salvation are evidenced in a life of good works. Jesus Himself told Nicodemus that we do not really see the wind—we just know that it's been by.

So, too, with salvation. We may not see it happen—but when it has, the works of a man saved by grace will shine through. Call it the lordship/salvation debate if you'd like. But if you remove the call to holy living from the gospel, or if you take it lightly, man may as well resort to a sacramental system to try to save himself. We would have only substituted a four-step formula for the sacramental system; either will allow a man to do his own thing. But the grace that saves also creates within man an otherworld desire to please and honor the God who so loved . . . and so gave.

Now I find myself a fully convinced evangelical—even though some evangelicals think I am still a Catholic. But I find that prejudice rooted deep within evangelicalism as well. Biblically, I often find myself confronting a mentality that says: "Catholics cannot be saved—because how can they be saved and remain within that system?" There the pain becomes real to me. . . .

So many Catholics seem turned off to the phrase *born again,* and we need to stop and admit that the way we evangelicals have approached them may have caused them to feel the way they do! Too many times we come at them—not just meet them—but come at them with a spiritual superiority . . . convinced categorically that all Cath-

olics are on their way to hell. Nothing could be further
from the truth. . . .

For those of you who may doubt my orthodoxy, please
know that I could not in any way step back into the Catholic Church as it is today. I do not believe in papal infallibility . . . the perpetual virginity of Mary . . . the
celebration of the Mass as a sacrifice for sin . . . the efficacy
of recited prayers . . . the doctrine of purgatory . . . and so
many others that have sprung up from an oral tradition
that subjects Scripture to the teaching of the church. But
many Catholics would not affirm those truths, either. Yet
that is still not the point. . . .

The fact of the matter is the typical evangelical in church
on Sunday morning is not terribly unlike the typical Roman Catholic at Mass. Let me explain.

The typical evangelical loves God as he understands
Him . . . seeks to worship Him with a corporate body on
a regular basis . . . desires his children to be instructed in
the love and laws of God . . . prays earnestly that his
children will be churchgoers who make a positive contribution to society . . . and—if we want to be painfully
truthful about this *typical* evangelical—does not want to be
terribly fanatical about such things as a separated life and
sharing the story of Christ with his neighbors and fellow
workers.

Now, just cross the street to the Catholic Church and we
will probably find the typical Catholic loves God as he
understands Him . . . seeks to worship Him with a corporate body on a regular basis . . . desires his children to
be instructed in the love and laws of God . . . prays earnestly that his children will be churchgoers who make a
positive contribution to society . . . and his parish priest
might say of this *typical* Catholic that he, too, probably has
no commitment to a separated life, nor does he feel any
compulsion to share the gospel with friend and neighbor.

We must willingly admit that a tremendous compla-
cency exists within Roman Catholicism and Evangelicalism. Yet in both groups, some men and women truly love
Jesus Christ as Lord and Savior . . . long to see Him

glorified in this life . . . desire to share Him with others that the whole world might know . . . and deeply feel the alienation that takes place among those who name themselves by the precious name of Christ.

As I think of Catholicism and Protestantism, images of the people I have known flash across my mind's screen. I think of individuals in both denominations, such as Father Harold Buckley, who radiated the love of Jesus and invested so much of his life in me when I was a troubled teen . . . Father Paul Vaeth, Passionist, whose commitment to Christ and pursuit of holiness challenges my own life and ministry . . . Father Terry Kristofak, Passionist, whose deep love for Jesus is evidenced in a desire to feed the hungry, clothe the naked, house the homeless, visit the imprisoned, and comfort the afflicted . . . Steve and Judy Hayes, who have built a marriage and a godly home on the unshakable foundation of Jesus their Lord . . . and Honey Breda, a devout Catholic laywoman whose love for the Master emanates from her total being as she seeks to be fed through the Bible study of an evangelical church and then returns to the challenge of being salt and light within her own parish. The list goes on and on. . . .

Within both camps God calls His people. He awakens people to the reality of Jesus alive . . . the Word made flesh and dwelling within men.

In the early sixties, a group of Catholic laymen in Pittsburgh began to pray about the lethargy they saw within their church, and their own lives. They cried out to heaven for a new Pentecost, and in a very real way, God spoke to that small band. From them has emitted a call to their Catholic brothers and sisters to come alive in Christ. They risked rejection and ridicule for the sake of the Christ to whom they had recently committed their lives, but they also made a commitment to remain within their own church for the purpose of preaching the gospel.

Because renewal had long concerned Catholic theologians, Ralph Martin and Stephen Clark wanted it to be understood from the beginning that they were not presenting another program—they wanted to present Jesus. Ralph Martin wrote these powerful words:

> The main thrust of renewal has proceeded on the basis of presupposing that the kerygma, the basic Christian message, had been effectively appropriated by the Christian people. What was needed, it was thought, was a theological updating that would centrally include a drawing out of the implications of Christianity for social action in the modern world. Another central focus of the renewal has been to work at the democratization of church structures. This, I believe, has had tragic results.
>
> The saving message, the kerygma, has not been effectively understood or appropriated by the Church as a whole. Countless millions of baptized Catholics in this country and others, have not personally committed their lives to Jesus, accepting Him as their Savior and Lord. Nor do they, despite the sacrament of confirmation, experience the effective power and working of the Holy Spirit in their lives.

Before you read on, why not read again those words penned, not by Billy Graham, or Bill Bright, or Bill Gothard—but a young Catholic layman: "Countless millions of baptized Catholics in this country and others, have not personally committed their lives to Jesus, accepting Him as their Savior and Lord."

What a confession—what a challenge to the Catholic Church! Who better to issue such a call then one within? I for one do not want to theologize with Ralph Martin or analyze his every word. I want to embrace him as a brother and sing praises with him to this Lord who has loved us . . . and saved us.

Steve Clark has made it so much easier for me to witness to Catholics. You see, some evangelicals look askance at me merely because I was a Catholic. At the same time, some Catholics will never trust me for that same reason. But for those who come to me for counseling—and many do—I delight in putting Steve's book before them . . . pointing out the imprimatur of Bishop Leo Pursley . . .

and then reviewing with them what Steve refers to as the Four Basic Truths. You may have seen similar ones in a little gold booklet printed by Campus Crusade for Christ. In Clark's book (*Team Manual for the Life in the Spirit Seminars* [Charismatic Renewal Services: 1972], 41–44.) they seem to find greater acceptance among Catholics. The medium itself is not really that important. The message is! Steve lays it out this way:

> Truth One: *God loves you and wants you to live a full happy life.*
> Truth Two: *Man is sinful and separated from God and therefore he cannot know God's love and share in God's life with others.*
> Truth Three: *Jesus Christ is the only one who can give you power to live this life. Through Him you can know God's love and share in God's life with others.*
> Truth Four: *You must accept Jesus Christ into your own life as Lord and Savior and you will receive the gift of the Holy Spirit who gives you power to live this new life.*

Clark makes it quite clear that each of these truths is based on the Word of God. He clearly spells out God's plan for a full and happy life in John 10:10. He speaks of the separation between man and God in the context of Romans 3:23 and Romans 1:28. He shares simply that Jesus is the only One, because God so loved the world that He sent His Son even as the Evangelist wrote in John 3:16. Finally, he makes it very clear that taking Christ as Lord means surrendering one's whole life. It is more than head knowledge—it goes beyond believing to receiving, just as we read in John 1:12.

That is pretty orthodox, and it ought to cause our hearts to sing and rejoice over what God is doing. It also ought to make us fall to our knees and pray that that proclamation will continue. Even more, it ought to raise up evangelical men and women who want to encourage born-again Catholics to grow in their love and knowledge of the Lord and His Word.

Several years ago, as the local congregations prepared to celebrate the Octave for Christian Unity, the ministers and priests were somewhat surprised when I told them I would like to be part of that week of prayer. I made it clear I wanted to work toward a greater understanding among those who call themselves Christians. More important, I needed them to understand that while I wanted to work toward the oneness for which Christ prayed on the night before He was killed, I could not be part of anything that smacked of an empty ecumenism that would deny the world's need for a Savior and rob the cradle and cross of the Godman.

They agreed that I could participate. I did *not* know of their intention to share pulpits. Later when I learned of it, my heart just about collapsed. I *knew* my elders would not be ready for that. . . .

Was I right! If we wanted to preach the gospel, what better way than within one of their congregations? I asked. Why could we not also allow one of those men who truly loved the Lord to come share his faith with us? I continued. Well, they certainly did like the idea of my preaching in one of *their* services on Sunday. But they reasoned, maybe it would be better if we invited one of the others to speak at our midweek service. I pointed out how unfair that really seemed. After much discussion, they agreed I could preach in one of the other churches on a Sunday morning, and one of the others, who truly loved the Lord, would be able to speak in our church that Sunday evening.

The Sunday within the Octave for Christian Unity happened to fall that year on a "holy day" in the church calendar known as Super Bowl Sunday. It seemed as if the experiment might be just a little safer still, because many of our people might not return for the evening service.

Between our two morning services, I dashed over to preach at the ten o'clock mass at Our Lady of Mercy. The pastor, Father Ken Herbster, is a dear friend. Together we bow to the lordship of Christ. So I found it exciting to be with him and his people. The time constraint was a little much for me—moving from a forty-five-minute message to a twelve to fifteen minute homily would be nothing short of a miracle. But it was such a special morning. At the end of those fifteen minutes his people stood spontaneously and began to applaud. No preaching experience had ever been so humbling for me . . . nor to this day, better received. I just talked about Jesus—and they listened attentively and eagerly.

That night, as most people geared up for a great football contest, I felt excited about the man who was going to preach to our people. You see, as it worked out, only Father Ken was willing to preach that Sunday evening. Our people knew the pastor of the local Catholic Church would speak. Many knew, too, this was quite probably the first time in the history of our denomination in America that a priest would be the preacher.

Ken's style is different from mine. He spoke softly and simply about his love for Christ . . . his understanding of divine forgiveness at Calvary . . . and the Father's love for this world for which He gave His Son. The congregation was hushed. (By the way, we had the largest evening attendance ever, short of Christmas Eve.) None of my people were aware of the reception I had received at Our Lady of Mercy that morning. But when Father Ken concluded his message, the Spirit of God so moved in the hearts of our people that they responded the same way, in spontaneous applause.

Ken Herbster knows all about the evangelical pastor who had been a Passionist. Neither suspicion nor mistrust has existed between us. Instead he has affirmed and loved me like a brother. We have shared our pain for the terrible fragmentation within the Body of Christ. That Sunday I most remember, at the service at Our Lady of Mercy, the kiss of peace Catholics share just before the communion service. As Ken invited his congregation to exchange that greeting, he walked down the steps of the altar, and with tears in both our eyes, we embraced. The tears said as much about our love for Christ and His church as also our feelings for each other.

This past Resurrection Morning, again with some concern on the part of our elders, Ken and I shared a sunrise service on the hillside adjoining our church. We gave a point-by-point sermon built on 1 Corinthians 15. Together

we preached resurrection reality and the need for all men
to commit themselves totally to the lordship of this One
who died on the cross for our sins and rose again. Though
the Catholics outnumbered us on the hillside, the fellowship that followed in our lower auditorium was sweet
indeed, as both churches—each somewhat afraid of the
other—learned of a common ground on which they might
build. But it takes much love and sensitivity; prejudices
and presuppositions must fall by the way.

Some might still struggle with my approach. I have not
written about papal infallibility, or the perpetual virginity,
or the Mass, or any other issue. My reason is simple—that
is not where most Catholics are at. If they were, approaching them on those grounds would be engaging in battle. I
am happy with making inroads—just the beginnings. My
chief concern in coming face to face with a Catholic is no
different from my concern for speaking to a complete
stranger whom I could meet on a plane tomorrow; I would
simply like to talk about Jesus. It is amazing where the
conversation will lead, if only our love for Christ and our
love for that individual can shine through. But I doubt many
people have been won to Christ in the head-on collision of
two strong-willed people convinced of what they believe.

In those early years of preparation for the priesthood,
two Latin words for "priest" struck me. The first, *pontifex*,
points to the role of the priest as a bridge builder. The
second, *sacerdos*, speaks of the holiness that ought to mark
his person.

Now, as an evangelical, I understand that all believers
are priests: "But you are a chosen race, a royal priesthood,
a holy nation, a people for God's own possession, that you
may proclaim the excellencies of Him who has called you
out of darkness into His marvelous light" (1 Peter 2:9).

That's us—a kingdom of priests. We need to see ourselves as a people given to the pursuit of holiness, but also
concerned enough about others that we try to tear down
the walls of suspicion and build bridges of understanding,
so that we can proclaim the excellencies of Christ, who
loved all men and gave Himself for them.